Parenting and the Internet

The Guide for Raising Your Child to Be Smarter and Safer Online

Todd Curtis

Speedbrake Publishing

Seattle, WA

Parenting and the Internet
The Guide for Raising Your Child to Be Smarter and Safer Online

Speedbrake Publishing
24 Roy St., #302
Seattle, WA 98109
USA
http://orders.speedbrake.com

All rights reserved. No part of this book may be reproduced, stored in an information or data retrieval system, or transmitted in any form, electronic, mechanical, photocopying, recording, or by any other means, without prior written permission from the author, except for the inclusion of brief quotations in a review.

Copyright © 2007 by Todd Curtis.

Printed in the United States of America.

Publisher's Cataloging-in-Publication
(Provided by Quality Books, Inc.)

Curtis, Todd, 1959–
    Parenting and the Internet: the guide for raising your child to be smarter and safer online / Todd Curtis. -- 1st ed.
    p. cm.
    Includes index.
    LCCN 2007922068
    ISBN-13: 978-1-887674-12-6 (softcover)
    ISBN-10: 1-887674-12-8 (softcover)
    ISBN-13: 978-1-887674-13-3 (PDF)
    ISBN-10: 1-887674-13-6 (PDF)

    1. Internet and children. 2. Parenting.
    3. Computers and family. I. Title.

HQ784.I58C87 2007   025.04'083
                             QBI07-600066

CONTENTS

Foreword 7
Acknowledgments 8
A Word from the Author 9
Warning — Disclaimer... 10

Chapter 1: Introduction... 11
    Who Is This Book For? 11
    What This Book Can Do for You 13
    How to Use This Book 14
    Conventions Used in This Book 16
    Additional Resources 18

Chapter 2: Parenting and the Internet................. 19
    Basic Philosophy.. 19
    Roles and Responsibilities................................. 22
    Q&A About Being an Online Parent............... 26

Chapter 3: Your Personal Computer..................... 29
    Personal Computer Hardware 30
    Personal Computer Software............................ 32
    Internet Service Providers 35
    Wireless or Wired Connection......................... 36
    Q&A About Home Computers......................... 37
    Top 10 Home Computer Accessories 39

Chapter 4: Privacy Online 41
    Key Privacy-related Threats.............................. 43
    Seven Steps to Online Privacy 48
    Recognizing a Privacy Problem....................... 73
    Top 10 Privacy Protection Tips........................ 74

Chapter 5: Security Online 75
    Key Security-related Threats............................ 78
    Seven Steps to Online Security 81
    Recognizing a Security Problem...................... 86
    Top 10 Security Protection Tips...................... 87

Chapter 6: Internet Legal and Ethical Issues 89
Copyrights and Trademarks 90
Pornography and Free Speech 95
Defamation and Libel Online 99
Ten Tips for Avoiding Online Defamation 100
Online Piracy 101

Chapter 7: Cyberbullies and Child Predators 103
Online Bullying 103
Cyberbullying Warning Signs 105
Top 10 Ways to Prevent Cyberbullying 107
Child Predators and the Internet 108
Law Enforcement Involvement 113
Top 10 Tips for Avoiding Online Predators 115

Chapter 8: Email Basics 117
An Overview of Email 118
Email Etiquette 125
The Gettysburg Criterion 126
Top 10 Email Realities 128

Chapter 9: Dealing with Unwanted Email 129
An Overview of Unwanted Email 130
Seven Steps to Controlling Email 132
Top 10 Ways to Stop Unwanted Email 141

Chapter 10: Web Basics 143
A Quick Overview of a Web Site 143
Basic Kinds of Web Sites 144
How to Use Search Engines and Directories 146
Top 10 Search Engine and Directory Tips 153
Finding the Key Sites on a Particular Subject 153
Top 10 Tips for Using the Web 161

Chapter 11: Avoiding Inappropriate Content 163
What Is Inappropriate Content? 163
Exposure to Inappropriate Content 164
Filtering Inappropriate Content 166
Seven Steps to Control Inappropriate Content 167
Top 10 Tips About Inappropriate Content 175

Chapter 12: Online at School and the Library 177
  Schools and the Internet 178
  Q&A About Being Online at School 179
  Top 10 Tips for Being Online at School 181
  Libraries and the Internet 182
  Q&A About Being Online at the Library 186
  Top 10 Tips for Being Online at the Library 188

Chapter 13: Beyond Email and the Web 189
  Instant Messaging 191
  Chat Rooms 192
  Social Networking 194
  Blogs 195
  Online Videos 197
  Photo Sharing 198
  File Sharing 199
  Webcams 200
  Podcasting 201

Chapter 14: Managing the Internet 205
  Setting Up Your Notebook 205
  Setting the Ground Rules 206
  Setting Up Your Home Computer 207
  Family Privacy Review 208
  Family Security Review 208
  Review of the Online Basics 208
  Things You Should Do Regularly 209
  The Stuff at the Back of the Book 209

Appendix 1: Free Software 211

Appendix 2: Online Resources 219

Appendix 3: Internet Use Agreements 247

Glossary 253

Index 277

Colophon 285

About the Author

Todd Curtis is a parent and a published author who more than a decade ago created the Web's most popular airline safety site, AirSafe.com. He holds a PhD in aviation risk assessment from the Union Institute, as well as engineering degrees from MIT, the University of Texas, and Princeton. His aviation safety work has been featured by numerous news organizations, including the New York Times, and he has appeared on CNN, CBS, Fox News, Discovery Channel, the BBC, and National Public Radio. With this book, he combines his insights as a father, engineering risk assessment expert, and online pioneer to create an easy-to-use guide for managing and enhancing a child's online experience. Previously, he has published a number of technical papers in the areas of airline safety and aviation risk assessment and authored the 2000 book *Understanding Aviation Safety Data*.

FOREWORD

The Internet is a valuable resource for parents and their children. The key message to parents is: you are in control—no matter whether your kids are more tech savvy than you—and you can feel more comfortable about your kids on the Internet when you know they know the rules. Your kids will feel as though they have a partner in learning when you make the effort to teach yourself about all the wonders of the Internet.

Your child needs to learn a number of technical skills to be able to go online, but he or she will also have to develop a number of social skills in order to use the Internet responsibly. Part of that social development is learning a set of values that will help to guide online behavior and activities in positive directions. With the leadership and values that you as a parent can provide, your child will be better able to avoid the hazards of the Internet and use the technology as a tool that will not only further his or her academic and social development, but also as a tool that will serve your family and community.

Trish Millines Dziko
Executive Director, Technology Access Foundation

Acknowledgments

There are numerous people from many fields who have helped to shape the advice and information in this book. Many online publishers have supported this effort with their advice and information, especially Mark Hasting and Leo Notenboom.

Educators and library professionals contributed as well, including Andra Addison, Nicole Stark, Sylvia Curtis, and Anna Renault.

Perhaps the most important group of contributors has been the many parents, grandparents, aunts, uncles, and cousins of online children. These adults have provided their questions, wishes, and sometimes cautionary tales during this book's development.

Special thanks go to Arlene Prunkl for editing, Robert Howard for cover design, and publishing consultant Faith Conlon. The most special thanks go to my wife, and especially to my son who regularly demonstrates just how much more I need to learn.

A Word from the Author

If you search any large bookstore for books about the Internet, you will find many how-to books on hardware, software, and the latest trends and gadgets, but very little about how to be a parent of an online child. While several books are available about the threats from online predators and some titles focus on parental control software, there are few books that address other concerns.

If you think there is more to being an online parent, this is the book for you. I've done my best to discuss key issues about being the parent of an online child that I do not see discussed in other books, issues that every parent needs to understand even before their child gets on the Internet for the first time. Topics include:

- How to make sure you control how your children use the Internet.
- Where to find all the free software and online resources you and your family will need to protect your computer and make it more useful.
- How to use online resources like search engines to help your child find useful information.
- How to protect your computer and your family from viruses and other malicious software.

No matter how much the technology of the Internet may change, or how your child's interests and needs change, this book will show you how to keep on top of it all and help your child become confident and capable online.

Dr. Todd Curtis, Seattle

WARNING—DISCLAIMER

This book is for informational purposes only. It is sold with the understanding that the publisher and author are not engaged in rendering legal or other professional services. If such assistance is required, you should seek the services of a competent professional.

It is not the purpose of this work to include all the information that is available, but to complement, amplify, and supplement other resources. You are urged to learn as much as possible about the subject matters covered, and to tailor the information to your individual needs.

Every effort has been made to make this book as accurate as possible. However, there may be mistakes both typographical and in content. Therefore, this text should be used only as a general guide on the subject matters covered. Furthermore, the information contained in this book was current only up to the printing date.

The purpose of this book is to educate and entertain. The author and publisher specifically disclaim any liability that is incurred, or that is alleged to have been caused, directly or indirectly, by the use or application of the contents of this book.

Any term appearing in this book that is known to be a trademark or service mark appears as requested by the owner of that mark. All names of products and services mentioned in this book are used in an editorial fashion only and to the benefit of the trademark or service mark owner, with no intention of infringement of any trademark or service mark. All trademarks and service marks are the property of their respective owners.

The fact that an organization or a web site is mentioned in this work as a source of information does not mean that the author or publisher endorses that organization or the recommendations it may provide. Also, you should be aware that web sites listed in this work may have changed or disappeared since this work was written.

If you do not wish to be bound by the above, please return this book to the publisher for a full refund.

CHAPTER 1

INTRODUCTION

In This Chapter
- Who Is This Book For?
- What This Book Can Do for You
- How to Use This Book
- Conventions Used in This Book
- Additional Resources

If you have picked up this book, you probably have a child who is on the Internet or will soon be online, and questions about how to manage your child's online experience. Even if you have been online yourself for years, you know that children approach the Internet differently from adults. This book deals with many of the issues that will arise, and will give you advice on how to set rules for online behavior, how to set up your computers, and how give your child the guidance he or she needs to be responsible online.

WHO IS THIS BOOK FOR?

This book is for anyone who is responsible in some way for a child who is on the Internet or about to be on the Internet. It is particularly useful for parents who have children in the home as well as a computer. The following brief sections have examples of the kinds of situations where this book will be helpful.

PARENTS WITH KIDS WHO ARE NOT YET ONLINE
Children often start using computers at a very young age, either at home or at school. For these children, computers are not a mystery, but simply things that are part of their normal lives. By the time your child is in elementary school, she will know about the Internet and will have an opportunity to go online or at least see others online.

PARENTS WHO WANT TO UNDERSTAND THE INTERNET
Figuring out the Internet can be a challenge, but with a little bit of effort you will learn enough to be able to ask the right questions and to make good decisions about your family's online activities. If you understand the basics of what the Internet is about, you will have the tools to be an effective online parent.

PARENTS WHO WANT MORE CONTROL OF THEIR ONLINE CHILD
No matter how much more your child knows about the Internet, your child is still a child and you are still a parent. Your rules must be the ones that matter, and you have to have enough control over your children's online activities to be able to protect them from online dangers.

PARENTS WHO WANT TO USE THE INTERNET FOR EDUCATION
Whether you homeschool your child or send your child to a traditional school, you can easily use the Internet to supplement your child's education by taking advantage of the resources of major libraries, or perhaps to read the local newspaper as well as newspapers from far away. With the guidance and information offered in this book,

Chapter 1—Introduction

you will be able to provide your children with many more tools that will help their formal education.

PARENTS WHO WANT MORE FROM THE INTERNET

There are more things to do online than you can imagine. The trick is figuring out which things are most important to you and finding out how to do those things online. There are many resources in this book that can get you started, and it also shows you how to go out and find what you need on your own.

WHAT THIS BOOK CAN DO FOR YOU

This book aims to be a basic guide for parents who want to get beyond the first hurdles of having their family and especially their children online. To get past those initial hurdles, this book will help you do several things:

- **Setting rules**: Every parent needs to have rules for their children regarding the use of the computer. The book has several suggestions for a written agreements that could be used with a young child, as well as agreements for older children.
- **Understanding basics**: Whether you have online experience or not, it is important that when your child goes online, she understands how to use a computer and how to use the basic Internet applications like email and search engines. Parents need to know enough about the kinds of online services children use so they can do a better job of making sure their children are acting responsibly online.
- **Finding good software**: Not only good software, but good free software. One of the great things

about the Internet is that there are communities of computer experts who have created free software for home computers. This book not only shows you where to find a lot of good, useful software, but it also provides resources that will let you find other free software that will work best for you.
- **Finding good resources**: The Internet has all kinds of free resources that your family can use right now, from help with homework and online dictionaries to medical information and science education. The book helps you here in two ways: by providing dozens of suggested resources as well as detailed instructions on how to find what you need online.
- **Keeping your family safe**: Identity thieves, online bullies, and child predators are just some of the hazards your child and your family face online. This book offers numerous detailed suggestions and guidelines you can use to reduce or eliminate most of these problems from your online lives.
- **Avoiding objectionable content**: It is no secret that the Internet has more than a few places your children should not visit. By following the advice given throughout this book, you can keep those uncomfortable and embarrassing moments to a minimum.

How to Use This Book

This book is designed to be used as a resource you can come back to again and again as your needs and the needs of your child change over time. Different parts of the book deal with the different needs you may have as a parent, no matter what kind of relationship you and your child have with the Internet. The following examples show how a general concern may be covered by different parts of the book:

- **Role of the parents**: Chapter 2 describes the philosophy behind this book, which is that parents are in charge and should take the lead in making the rules about what their children can do online.
- **Setting up your computer**: Whether you already have a computer at home or you plan on getting one soon, chapter 3 tells you what a basic setup looks like and what kind of software and hardware extras you may need. Appendix 1 also contains descriptions of many kinds of free software you can add at any time.
- **Maintaining privacy**: Chapter 4 describes how easy it is for your family's privacy to slip away if you and your children are not careful online. The chapter also has plenty of advice on keeping a low online profile and for creating passwords and user names to protect your privacy.
- **Staying secure online**: Chapter 5 gives you a basic review of online safety issues for families, while chapter 7 addresses both online bullying and child predators.
- **Using email and the Web**: This is a big subject, but an important one for children learning how to use the Internet. Chapters 8 and 9 discuss how to use email and also how to avoid unwanted email, while chapters 10 and 11 discuss how to find good information and resources online while avoiding objectionable content.

- **Rules you should know**: Parents need to know how to keep themselves and their children out of trouble when going online at home, at school, and at the library. Chapter 6 explains some of the basic legal realities of being online, while chapter 12 discusses common online rules at schools and libraries.
- **Online activities you should know about**: Kids adapt to change easily, and the enticing new features on the Internet are no exception. Before your kid dives into a new online activity, you need to decide if it is a good idea or one you and your child should pass up. Several popular online activities are covered in chapter 13, including social networking, chat rooms, instant messaging (IM), photo sharing, blogging, and podcasting.
- **Managing your child's activities**: Chapter 14 gives you an easy-to-follow plan for setting up your household to make it easy to keep track of all the things your child does online, including all of their online accounts, all of their passwords, and all of their data.
- **Handy reference material**: The back of the book includes a glossary of computer and Internet terms in plain English, as well as lists of useful free software and free online resources.

CONVENTIONS USED IN THIS BOOK

COMPUTER EXAMPLES

This book assumes that you will be using computers that run the Windows XP operating system, along with one or both of the most popular browsers, Internet Explorer and

Firefox. Some of the Internet Explorer examples are specific either to version 6 or version 7, and all of the Firefox examples are specific to version 2.

INSTRUCTIONS

When step-by-step instructions are provided for changing settings on a computer application, the title of a window, of a group of instructions, or of a specific command will be in **bold text**. A sequence of commands will be in bold and separated by a greater-than mathematical symbol (for example, **Start> All Programs> Accessories> Notepad**).

CAPITALIZATION

When a company's specific software programs are mentioned, those names will be capitalized. The word *Internet* will always be capitalized, as will the phrase *World Wide Web* or the abbreviation *Web*. However, phrases referring to something other than the entire World Wide Web will be in lowercase. These would be phrases like *web site* or *web page*. The capitalized word *Windows* refers to the operating system software from the Microsoft Corporation, but the lowercase word *window* refers to rectangular spaces on a computer display.

GLOSSARY TERMS

At their first occurrence, words and phrases related to computers or the Internet are usually explained in the text. If an important term is not defined in a chapter, you will find the definition in the glossary in the back of the book.

ADDITIONAL RESOURCES

The free Family Forms Pack is available online at http://forms.speedbrake.com. This document contains all the forms and family Internet agreements mentioned in the book, as well as information bonuses such as extended how-to guides along with related audio and video instructions. You can also visit the *Parenting and the Internet* podcast page at http://podcast.speedbrake.com to hear about new developments that affect families with online children.

Feel free to contact the publisher if you have any questions or comments about the book. Any stories you have about how the book helped you and your family would be particularly welcome. Write to:

> Dr. Todd Curtis
> c/o Speedbrake Publishing
> 24 Roy St., #302
> Seattle, WA 98109
> feedback@speedbrake.com
> http://feedback.speedbrake.com

CHAPTER 2

PARENTING AND THE INTERNET

In This Chapter
- Basic Philosophy
- Roles and Responsibilities
- Q&A About Being an Online Parent

If you are now a parent, you probably first learned how to use the Internet at school or in the workplace, controlled environments with rules of online behavior enforced by teachers or managers. This is quite different from today, where your child is much more likely to learn about the Internet while at home. If this is the case, you will have to take a very active role in teaching your child how to use the Internet.

BASIC PHILOSOPHY

The basic philosophy of this book is simple—parents should be in control and take the lead regarding making the rules about how children use computers and the Internet. There is simply no other way of running a household with children. Allowing the children to make all the decisions about how or when to use a computer makes about as much sense as allowing a child to make all the decisions about how and when to drive a car. Just as is the case with a car, a child may be highly motivated and may even have superior skills when it comes to driving and maintaining a car. However, a child does not have the experience, the judgment, or the level of responsibility that a parent has. Technology has to take a back seat to parenting.

MY PARENTS AND THEIR TEENAGE DRIVERS
The situation that you face as a parent with the Internet in the 21st century is similar to what my parents faced with cars in the 20th century. My parents were teenagers in the early 1940s when it was rare for the average teenager, including both of my parents, to have the use of a car. When I was old enough to drive, there was never any question about whether my parents were justified in telling me when I could drive, where I could drive, and how I could drive. It did not matter that they never drove cars as teenagers.

My parents' authority over my driving did not depend on their technical skills. I was much more knowledgeable about cars than my mother. I knew how to fill the tank, change a tire, and even hot-wire my 1964 Ford Falcon, which were all things my mother could not do. Did she let the fact that I knew more about cars keep me from following her rules, whether I liked it or not? Not at all.

Your Technological Generation Gap
Don't feel left out because you were not online as a child. Chances are, you are too old! The first time computers were ever connected using the technology of the Internet was in 1969, email was first introduced in 1972, and the first browser in 1990.

Cars, Computers, and Parenting

As was the case with previous generations, it should not matter if you used a particular technology as a child. You are still a parent, and you have to make the kinds of decisions parents make in every generation. When it comes to the Internet, it does not matter whether you are a computer expert who has been online for more than 20 years or if you don't know the first thing about computers. Being online is a very important part of modern life, and one way or another it will be a very important part of your child's life.

Think of computers and the Internet the same way you would treat cars, televisions, cell phones, or any other technology you use. You do not have to understand *how* any of these technologies work to understand how to make them work for you. If you allow your child to use these technologies, you are also responsible for making sure your child uses them in a safe, sensible, and responsible manner.

Why the Internet Is Different

While the Internet represents a technology, it is different in some important ways from other technologies like cars, phones, television, and even personal computers:

- **Community**: By using the Internet, your family becomes part of a much larger community, and learning how to deal with that community is an ongoing process for your entire family.
- **Communication**: The tools and services of the Internet allow you and your child to communicate in ways that are very different from what you are used to, and you have to understand how those

differences can either help or hurt you or your child.
- **Change**: The things that are available online change very quickly, with many new or more sophisticated services being offered every year.
- **Culture**: The Internet has become a normal part of everyday life, with most children using it at home, in school, or at the library well before they reach middle school. As a parent, you have little choice but to learn how to deal with it in your child's life.

WHY THE INTERNET IS NOT DIFFERENT

The Internet is not magic or mysterious. It is merely one of the many technologies that families deal with every day. As with any other technology, a family has to decide how much or how little a role it plays in the family's life. The Internet can give a family greater options and greater opportunities if the family members, particularly the parents, are willing to make the decisions and take the actions that are sensible and necessary. If you are willing to do those things, the Internet will be a very positive thing in your family's life.

ROLES AND RESPONSIBILITIES

One of the core themes of this book is that parents must take the lead in guiding a child's development on the Internet. Because using the Internet can be at times complicated, with your child able to perform several online activities at the same time, your involvement as a parent will be much different than your involvement with your child using a simpler technology like television.

ROLE OF THE PARENTS

The following are this book's basic assumptions about the role of parents:

- **Parents are the leaders**: Within the family, the parents are responsible for providing guidance and boundaries when it comes to a child's use of the Internet, and for making sure that a child's online behavior reflects the family's values. Written agreements such as the examples given elsewhere in the book give both you and your child common reference points when dealing with the Internet.
- **Parents make the decisions**: In any significant decision involving a child's online activities, parents must have the final say, such as whether to allow a computer in the home, what hardware or software should be installed on the computer, or what activities are allowed online.
- **Parents make and enforce the rules**: As a parent, you have to set limits on what your children do online. Those include limits on when a child can be online, what he can do online, and who he communicates with online. These parental roles are necessary no matter what technology may be involved.
- **Parents guide children toward independence**: Eventually your child will want or need to go online without you at his side. You must anticipate this and work with him, knowing that one of your goals is to make sure he will in time become competent and knowledgeable enough to go online alone.

- **Parents provide values as well as skills**: While ensuring that order and discipline govern a child's online activities, parents should also teach and enforce basic values that have meaning beyond the entertainment or education that is offered by the technology of the Internet.

ROLE OF THE CHILD

Your child's role in proper Internet use is very similar to her role in the family. A child will start off needing the close support and supervision of a parent, but eventually she will develop emotionally and intellectually, as well as become more sophisticated in the use of technology. All these things would be very difficult without the close involvement of parents. Some of a child's more important roles include the following:

- **Children must play by their parents' rules**: What works in the rest of a child's life also works on the Internet. If your child is not willing to play by your rules, you impose restrictions. Because being online is something that kids generally enjoy, denying access as a consequence of poor behavior often serves as a big incentive for her to change that behavior.
- **Children must be responsible for their actions**: Your child must know that when she is online, actions have consequences. You need to make it clear what she can do online, and you should also be prepared to take appropriate actions when she does not live up to her responsibilities.
- **Children must share their experience**: It is no secret that kids think and act differently from

adults in many areas of life, including their use of the Internet. Even if you have years of online experience, you could likely learn many new things from your child. Encourage your child to share her online experience so you can both learn together.
- **Learning about the Internet is a key goal**: No child knows exactly how the Internet will fit into her life. It is important that your child learns as much as she can about the basics of the Internet and how to make it both useful and entertaining.

INTERNET USE AGREEMENTS AND YOUR CHILD

One of the best things you can do to make the whole process easier is to put things in writing, starting with a written agreement on the use of the Internet. Having a written contract between you and your child may seem to be an extreme measure, but your opinion may change as you go through this book. You will see that being an online parent means keeping track of many different things, including what is acceptable behavior and what is not. Writing things down reduces the confusion and gives both you and your family a starting place as all of you figure out what kind of relationship your family will have with the Internet.

If you would like to look at some sample Internet use agreements, you will find them in appendix 3. After going through some of the other chapters in the book, you may find that you will want to add to or subtract from what you see in these sample agreements.

ONLINE FAMILY VALUES

The sample agreements in appendix 3 include something that is rarely discussed in books and articles about the Internet: the role of values. The combination of personal computers and the Internet is a powerful tool, and the potential for that tool to expand your child's world is limited only by the imagination. What your child does online will be influenced by values expressed by schools, classmates, and others outside of your family. It is up to you to make sure the values that are important to your family shape what your child does online.

You probably have many different values that you would like your child to take to heart, but your family Internet use agreement should focus on the one or two values you think are the most important. When you sit down with your child to talk about the online agreement, it would also be a good time to talk about what those values are and to put them in writing.

Q&A ABOUT BEING AN ONLINE PARENT

Why should I have a written contract with my child?
It is important your child understands that being online has many important consequences, and that you have expectations of how she will behave. It also shows her you are serious about issues like her safety online. Most importantly, it will show your child that you plan on being involved in what she does online.

The Internet seems so complicated to me. How am I supposed to learn about all that stuff?
You don't have to understand the entire Internet to be able to use it. It is like anything else involving technology;

you learn enough to get started, and you get better at it as you go along.

My kid knows so much more about the Internet, and I feel like I won't ever be able to catch up.
That may be true, but you still must act like a parent when it comes to computers and the Internet. Think of the computer and the Internet as tools, or even as a kind of household appliance. Even if your child knows much more than you about how a tool or appliance works, you must use your common sense to figure out whether it is being used properly or not.

How do I explain to my son why I am making rules about how to use the Internet?
Explain why you are making the rule, and one of two things will happen: either he will understand your reasoning and follow the rule, or he will not. If he does not understand your reasons, arguing will probably not change that, so save your energy. Saying "because I say so" is a good enough response.

What is an important value to have in the family Internet agreement?
That is a question only you can answer. Think of an idea or a goal that sustains your family in good times and bad, no matter what kinds of distractions, temptations, and roadblocks get in your way. Talk about it with your family, and I'm sure that all of you will come up with several ideas.

Free Software that Works for Me

I have featured free software in throughout this book because I regularly use many of those same programs. Among the free programs I regularly use are the Firefox browser, iTunes media player, and every piece of software used to create the *Parenting and the Internet* podcasts.

Chapter 3

Your Personal Computer

In This Chapter
- Personal Computer Hardware
- Personal Computer Software
- Internet Service Providers
- Wireless or Wired Connection
- Q&A About Home Computers
- Top 10 Home Computer Accessories

The one thing your child will need to go online is a computer. If you don't have one in your home and would like to get a new one, you need to know a little about what you'll have to buy. If you already have one, then you should have some idea about whether you need to add any hardware or software, or whether you need to get a new computer.

Computers and the Internet may be complicated technologies, but you don't have to be some kind of technical genius to understand the basics. Let me make another car analogy: think of computers and the Internet the way you think of driving. Cars are complex pieces of machinery and you have to share the road with millions of other drivers, but you can drive a car without knowing how to build a car, and you don't have to know every traffic rule for every situation in order to drive safely.

If you can understand the basic facts in this chapter, you will have enough information to at least ask the right questions about what you may need to get you and your child online.

Personal Computer Hardware

The two most common types of personal computers used in homes are desktop computers and laptop computers. Laptops are also known as notebook computers. Both kinds of computers have the same basic components, with the laptop putting all those components into one portable unit and the desktop having those components connected by wires and cables. Some basic components are included in even the cheapest desktop and laptop computers, and there are other components that you will probably want to add to make the computer more useful.

Basic Personal Computer Components

The following components are usually included with every new desktop or laptop:

- **CD-ROM Drive**: This component can read or write data to or from a CD-ROM. Software is often sold and distributed by CD-ROM.
- **CPU**: Also known as the central processing unit, this is the brain of the computer that uses software and inputs from the user in order to operate. For a desktop computer, this term also refers to the component containing all the basic hardware, including the hard drive.
- **Display**: Laptop computers and most new desktop computers come with a flat screen display that

uses the same kind of technology as a flat screen television.
- **Hard drive**: This is where most of the information on the computer is stored, including software and data. Information is stored in files, which are organized collections of data that can be saved or retrieved by a computer.
- **Keyboard**: This has the same basic keys and layout as a typewriter, with a number of other keys for various computer-related functions.
- **Modem**: This is a device that allows the computer to communicate with the Internet through either a telephone line, cable connection, or wireless connection.
- **RAM**: Short for random access memory, this is the area of the computer where data is temporarily stored when the computer is operating.

OPTIONAL BUT VERY USEFUL HARDWARE

The following pieces of hardware are not standard equipment that come with most new computers, but your computer will be much more useful if you have them:

- **DVD drive**: DVDs have a much higher data capacity than a CD-ROM. This kind of drive is most useful if it also has a writing capacity.
- **External hard drive**: This is an independent hard drive that can be connected to a computer. Typically, this kind of drive has much greater capacity than other portable data storage devices.
- **Flash drive**: This is another kind of portable data storage device.

- **Mouse**: This is a device that can position the cursor and select items on the screen. Most laptops have one built into the keyboard, but for many people an external mouse is easier to use. You could run the computer using only the keyboard, but it is usually easier to use a mouse with the keyboard.
- **Printer**: Typically, you can use this to print documents either in black and white or in color.
- **Router**: This is a device you need to use if you want to create a home wireless network that allows computers in your home to connect to the Internet without using cables or wires.
- **Speakers**: Some online content contains audio. Although you could use headphones or built-in speakers, external speakers usually give a much higher sound quality.
- **Surge suppressor**: This electrical accessory is designed to protect sensitive electronic devices from sudden and significant changes in voltage; for example, from a power outage.
- **Wireless modem**: This kind of modem allows the computer to connect to the Internet without using wires or cables.
- **Writable CD-ROM drive**: A basic CD-ROM drive can only read data, but a writable drive can also save data onto a writable CD-ROM.

Personal Computer Software

Most of the software you will need either comes with your computer, or else can be easily obtained. Fortunately, many of the additional programs you and your family are likely to use are often available for free.

Basic Personal Computer Software

The following programs are included with every new desktop or laptop, and you will use them every time you go online:

- **Browser**: This kind of software program allows your computer to interpret, display, or access information from the Internet.
- **Email program**: This kind of program allows you to compose, send, and receive email messages.
- **Operating system**: This program controls all the other software that operates in the computer and any devices connected to the computer.

Optional but Very Useful Software

The following types of software may or may not come with your machine, but free software that can perform each of the following functions can be found online:

- **Antispyware**: This software can detect or remove spyware from a computer, or prevent spyware from being installed.
- **Antivirus**: Software designed to detect or remove software viruses from a computer.
- **Firewall**: This software controls communications between a personal computer and the Internet and prevents unauthorized access to that computer.
- **PDF reader**: This software allows the display of files in the Portable Document Format, a file type widely used to distribute documents online.
- **Photo organizer**: This type of software can be used to manage photos and other graphics files.

- **Presentation manager**: This software is used to create, display, and print presentations that may use a combination of text, graphics, and audio.
- **Spreadsheet**: This kind of software will display data in one or more rectangular grids, and allows the user to perform calculations on that data.
- **Word processor**: This software allows a user to create, edit, format, display, and print documents containing both text and graphics.

Optional but Entertaining Software

It is no secret that children enjoy and adults having fun on the computer, especially with music, movies, or video games. Perhaps the best way to make your computer into a part-time entertainment center is to add general-purpose media player software that will allow your computer to play music CDs, DVDs, and multimedia files in other formats. Most new computers come with some kind of media player software, and there are several types of media player programs that can be downloaded for free. The "Media Software" section of appendix 1 includes several options for audio and video players.

Free Software vs. Purchased Software

When you buy a personal computer, it will likely not have all of the software that you will want or need. New software can be very expensive, with some of the more sophisticated programs costing hundreds of dollars. While you may have to buy some programs, you have plenty of options for free software that can perform many of the functions that you or your child may want your computer to do

Many of the free software products mentioned in this

book were created by for-profit companies. In some cases, the company has more advanced versions of the software that must be purchased, and the less capable free software acts as a marketing tool. Other companies give away the software in order to encourage you to buy other products and services. Some free programs were developed by organizations staffed by volunteers who also provide free support. Whatever the motivation of the creators, your family can benefit by using free programs whenever you have the opportunity.

INTERNET SERVICE PROVIDERS

You must use the services of an Internet Service Provider (ISP) if you want to access the Internet from your home computer. One of your first tasks after getting a new home computer will be to decide what kind of Internet connection you want. Most ISPs will offer you one or more of the following options:

- **Dial-up**: This is Internet connection through a telephone line. You cannot connect to the Internet and use your telephone for voice communication at the same time. Typically, this is the cheapest and slowest kind of online connection.
- **DSL (Digital Subscriber Line)**: This Internet access option allows a higher connection speed than dial-up, and also uses a standard phone line. Unlike a dial-up connection, a user can make and receive voice telephone calls while simultaneously connected to the Internet.

- **Cable modem**: This connection to the Internet uses a coaxial cable that may also carry other data such as television programming.

WIRELESS OR WIRED CONNECTION

When you choose higher speed Internet connection options such as DSL or cable modem, you have the option of having your personal computer directly wired into the connection, or using additional hardware and software to allow wireless connections to the Internet.

Whether you choose a wireless or wired connection depends on your situation. If you only have a single desktop computer, then a wireless connection may not make sense. However, if you have several computers in your home and more than one of them may be in use at the same time, then it may be practical to have a wireless connection.

WIRELESS ISSUES

Two issues have to be addressed if you choose wireless: the issue of wireless security and the issue of managing your child's online activities. The first is easily addressed by using the available security features that are built into a typical wireless system. More details are provided in the section "Seven Steps to Online Privacy" in chapter 4.

The second issue may be more complicated. With a wireless system in a household, a computer can be set up wherever it is convenient. Make sure the computer your child uses is placed in a position where you and other family members can easily see what is happening on or near the computer. If your child is using a laptop, then you may have to include additional rules outlining where the laptop must be located whenever your child is online.

Q&A About Home Computers

Which is better, a desktop or a laptop computer?
It depends on your family's needs. If the computer will always be in the same location in your home, then get the desktop. If you need to be able to move it around your home, then the laptop makes more sense.

What do I need to go online?
Your new computer will come installed with a browser and several options for going online. You need a regular telephone line to access the Internet for most providers. If you want to set up your home for wireless access, you will need additional hardware such as a wireless router.

How much does it cost to go online?
Basic dial-up access plans can start from less than $10 per month. High-speed access using DSL or cable modem will cost more. Most areas have several choices for service, so compare offers and pick the one that is best for you.

What extra equipment should I buy with my computer?
The one extra that almost everyone needs is a printer. If you have a laptop, it should be equipped with wireless networking capability. Speakers usually come with a new computer, but the quality may not be that great, especially for laptops. If you want to have your computer function as a music and entertainment center, you may want to get better speakers.

Does my hardware have to be from the same company?
No, it doesn't. You can use printers, speakers, keyboards, and other accessories that come from other companies.

How much is a new computer?
That depends on what kind of computer you want and what kind of extras you want to have. In 2007, prices for new desktop computers (with display included) from major manufacturers started from below $400 and new laptops from below $500.

Where is the best place to get a new computer?
You can go to consumer electronics stores, or even large department stores to buy a computer, or you can order one online or by phone. Some companies do not sell their computers through retail outlets and others allow you to buy a computer in traditional stores or online. No matter where you buy a computer, make sure that you buy it from a company that has a good reputation for customer service.

What extras do I need to buy to play music and videos?
Most new computers should come with media software, or you can download a program for free. If anyone in your family plans to have a lot of music or video on the computer, then two other useful extras are a DVD drive and a larger-capacity hard drive.

How fancy should my new computer be?
A basic personal computer will come with the Windows operating system already installed (in 2007, that would be either Windows XP or Windows Vista), along with enough software and hardware to be able to connect to the Internet. You really don't need to buy extra software–since all the basic software you'll need to do work for home, for school, or for a small business can be found online for free (see chapter 14 and appendix 1 for details).

Can I afford a computer on a limited budget?
Let's put it this way. A new computer and a year's worth of Internet access costs less than a television with a year's worth of cable access, a video game system with a handful of new games, ten cartons of cigarettes, or a weekend stay at a theme park. That computer will probably do much more for you, for your child, and for your family than any of those other things. If your family budget is limited, cut something else out and get that computer.

Where is the best place in my home to put a computer?
If you have only a single computer and if it will stay in one place, keep it in a part of your home where you and other family members can easily drop by and look at what your children are doing online. If you have a wireless connection and laptop computers, insist that your children can only go online if the computer is in an open area where others can see what is going on. No matter what your situation, your child should not be allowed to go online behind closed doors.

TOP 10 HOME COMPUTER ACCESSORIES

If you are about to get a new or used computer for your home, make sure you also have the following extra software and hardware accessories. You do not need them to use the computer, but they make using the computer or using the resources of the Internet so much easier. Refer to appendix 1 for details on where to get the free software mentioned in this list.

1. **Printer**: You can use this to make paper copies of documents from files on your computer or from online resources.

2. **Mouse**: You can run every program on your computer using the keyboard or a built-in mouse, but most programs and web sites are much easier to use if you use an external mouse.
3. **Writable CD-ROM drive**: Having this capacity makes it easy to store data or to create music CDs using relatively inexpensive CD-ROMs
4. **External speakers**: Most laptops and even some desktops have built-in speakers, but a pair of external speakers, even very cheap ones, will give you a much better-quality sound.
5. **Flash drives**: You can use these either as a way to back up your files or to transfer files between computers.
6. **Firefox browser**: This alternative to Internet Explorer allows a user to have more control over the browsing experience, especially when it comes to blocking advertising.
7. **OpenOffice.org**: This office application suite has all the software you need for doing word processing, spreadsheets, and presentations for either work or school.
8. **Adobe Reader**: This software can be used to view, print, and search PDF files, which is the preferred file format for many online documents.
9. **Google Desktop**: This program allows you to search for content on your computer's hard drive in the same way you do online searches with the Google search engine.
10. **iTunes media player**: You can use this program to easily manage most of the audio and music files on your computer, and you do not have to buy an iPod to use the software.

CHAPTER 4

PRIVACY ONLINE

In This Chapter
- Key Privacy-related Threats
- Seven Steps to Online Privacy
- Recognizing a Privacy Problem
- Top 10 Ways to Protect Your Privacy Online

The Internet is a very social medium. In the United States, more than half of the adult population regularly goes online, and an even larger percentage of teens and preteens make the Internet a regular habit. Part of the habit includes taking steps to protect your privacy. If you don't, you could face all kinds of privacy problems, from junk emails to online predators. Parents have two key roles in protecting their children's privacy, helping them to develop good online habits, and taking steps to make sure that any computer or online service that a child uses is set up to protect that child's private information.

WHAT DOES PRIVACY MEAN?

A simple definition of privacy in this context is the ability to control the type and amount of access others have to your personal information and the amount of control you allow others to have over your online experience.

Why Online Privacy Is Important

Keeping private and personal information under control is important to anyone who spends time online. If you or your family do not take steps at least some basic steps to protect your online privacy, you may be at increased risk from one or more of the following privacy-related hazards:

- Being sent large amounts of unsolicited email.
- Becoming a victim of identity theft.
- Exposure to large amounts of online advertising
- Unauthorized access to your computer or to an online account.
- Unauthorized bank or credit card activity.

Examples of Private Information

Private information includes any information about your life or about your child's life that you would like to control. This is information that in the wrong hands could bring unwanted attention or that could put you or your child at emotional, financial, or physical risk. A partial list of that kind of information would include the following:

- Age
- Birth date
- Current or former address
- Current or former employers
- Current or former phone numbers
- Current or former schools
- Email addresses
- Financial information
- Gender

- Information needed to access computers, computer networks, or online services
- Lifestyle information such as travel schedules, group affiliations, clubs, favorite activities, and details about personal relationships
- Medical information
- Mother's maiden name
- Name, nickname, or initials
- Social Security number or other information from government-issued identification

KEY PRIVACY-RELATED THREATS

Your family's privacy is at risk when others get too much access to your private information or when others get too much control over the information that gets sent to you. While some of the following types of privacy problems are caused by outsiders, others can be caused by your online habits or by those of your child.

FRAUDULENT SCHEMES

There are several kinds of fraudulent schemes where obtaining privacy-related information is just the first step of a possible crime. Some examples include the following:

- **Credit card fraud**: This is any kind of a scheme where the criminal gets someone to volunteer credit card information in order to make bogus or unauthorized charges.
- **Identity theft**: The unauthorized use of personal information in order to take on the identity of another person.
- **Other scams and cons**: There are a number of other criminal schemes in which the goal of the criminal

is to gain the confidence of someone over a period of time before the actual crime occurs. These kinds of threats are usually aimed at adults rather than children. Examples include fake lotteries, bogus requests to help transfer funds to a bank account, and stock investing schemes.
- **Pharming**: This is a technique used by identity thieves and other criminals in which traffic is redirected from a legitimate web site to a fake site, where the potential victim is then encouraged to provide personal or financial information.
- **Phishing**: This is a technique by which a bogus email, web site, or popup message appears to be a legitimate request for private information such as your name, Social Security number, or online account information.

Hardware Issues

Privacy may be compromised if the personal data stored on a computer is stolen or if the computer is given away or sold to with personal data still on the hard drive. Similar risks exist for lost or stolen data on portable storage media such as a CD-ROM or a flash drive.

Intrusive or Excessive Advertising

One way advertisers control the type or amount of advertising that you or your child may see on a web site is through the use of cookies. These are small text files that a web site you are visiting places on your computer. They allow your browser to retain information about your web site visit. When you make a return visit, the web site may show specific advertising based on the data in the cookie.

Another way advertising may intrude on your online

experience is through a popup. This is a type of browser window that automatically appears on top of the current browser window during a visit to a particular web page. Popups do not by themselves cause harm, but they are often associated with aggressive advertising methods.

PERSONAL DATA IN YOUR SOFTWARE

Many of the programs on your personal computer may allow you to add personal information such as your name, address, and telephone number. Each time you send someone a file, that data is also included.

HAZARDS OF HOME WIRELESS NETWORKS

Unless you have taken the time to secure your wireless network, anyone with a wireless-ready computer will be able to use it, including hackers who may use that connection to access the information on your computer. Also, if an unauthorized person uses your network to access the Internet, commit a crime, or perform activities that violate your ISP's terms of service, your ISP may take actions to freeze or cancel your account.

MALICIOUS SOFTWARE THREATS

Malicious software is any software designed to cause harm to a computer or the person using it. There are two general types of malicious software that may cause you to lose control over your personal information or that allow intrusive advertising on your computer:

- **Adware**: This type of software allows advertising to appear while you are online and possibly when you are not online.

- **Spyware**: This kind of software collects data about your computer and your online activities and sends the information to someone else without your permission or knowledge.

Personal Behavior

Online habits and personal computer habits can directly affect the privacy risks that you and your family may face. Some of the more common risks that are due to personal behavior include the following:

- **Not sending sensitive data in a secure way**: The most sensitive kind of personal data is the kind that can lead to identity theft and financial loss.
- **Publicly displaying personal information**: Some services encourage users to place personal data onto a web page. Once there, this information is available to anyone who wishes to see it.
- **Responding to requests for personal information**: You and your child will likely receive requests for personal information. If there is no way to verify that a request is legitimate, responding in any way may lead to privacy problems.
- **Volunteering personal information**: Although you may be asked to provide personal information when using an online service or registering a product, there is usually no requirement to do so. Once you give out this information, it may be used to direct advertising and unsolicited offers to you or to your child.

How Much Privacy Should a Child Have?

You should take all reasonable steps to allow your child some personal privacy, but you should always be able to get access to any of your child's online accounts and to any data in a computer or in a portable storage device.

Key Realities About Privacy

If you are always at your child's side when he or she is online, privacy will not be an issue since you will have complete control over any online activities. An older child may resist this kind of parental access, but any argument your child may give you has to be considered in light of the following realities:

- **No one has total privacy online**: Just about any email, instant message, or other communication has to pass through an ISP, and will also likely pass through several computer systems on the journey between the sender and receiver. Your ISP can also keep records of every site you or your child may visit.
- **Parents are responsible for their child's safety**: Every child should have the ability to keep some things private, and parents should respect those needs. However, when it comes to issues involving a child's online behavior or personal safety, parents have a responsibility to intervene.
- **Privacy is not the same as secrecy**: Parents and children must learn how to respect each other's privacy. However, the role of a parent will always be different from the role of a child. If a parent needs to go into a child's room, the parent may out of respect for the child knock on the door and ask

to enter, but if a child says no, a responsible parent will still go in. Ultimately, children do not have the right to keep information secret from their parents if the parents have a legitimate need to know.

SEVEN STEPS TO ONLINE PRIVACY

Prevention is your best option for establishing control of private information and curbing excessive intrusions into your online experience. Many of the current threats can be addressed with a combination of appropriate technology and sensible online and offline behavior. The technology component of privacy involves both your home computer and the online services you may use. Your family's online behavior contributes to your privacy by steering you away from situations that put privacy at risk. You and your family should heed the following suggestions to enhance your privacy:

1. Develop a family privacy protection plan.
2. Set up your hardware and software to limit or prevent unauthorized activity.
3. Add software designed to protect your privacy.
4. Adopt online habits that protect your personal and private information.
5. Create and use an online alias.
6. Respond appropriately to information requests.
7. Regularly review your family's online activities.

STEP 1: HAVE A FAMILY PRIVACY PROTECTION PLAN

Chapter 2 discussed the role of your child's written Internet use agreement and how it forms the foundation of how you and your child will deal with online issues. Appendix 3 provides an example of a basic agreement for a child who will only be online with a parent and another example of an agreement for a child who can go online alone. The following elements should be included in the agreement if your child will only be online if supervised by you or by another adult:

- I will not go online alone. If I am online, I must be with a parent or another responsible person.
- If my parents say that I can't do something on the computer, I will obey them.

If your child is allowed to go online alone, the agreement should include the following:

- I will not give out my name, address, telephone number, or any other personal information about my family or myself to anyone online without my parents' permission.
- I will not hide anything about what I do online from my parents. If my parents ask, I will let them look at any file I have on any computer, in any online account, or on any data storage device.
- I will not order or buy anything online without getting my parents' permission.
- I will not post anything online without my parents' permission.
- I will not download any file without getting my parents' permission.
- I will not send a picture or other file to anyone else unless I get my parents' permission.
- I will tell my parents the user name, password, or any other information they need to get into any online account or online service that I have.

STEP 2: SET UP YOUR HARDWARE AND SOFTWARE

The typical home computer system has privacy-related features that have to be activated in order to be effective. Activating these features will not prevent all privacy-related problems, but it could make your family's online experience more enjoyable by limiting some kinds of privacy hazards. There are at least three kinds of changes you can make to your system:

1. Use the privacy options included in your browser to control how cookies and popups are handled.
2. Set up your wireless network by turning on privacy features that will make it more difficult for people outside your family to access your system.
3. Ensure that the applications on your computer do not include privacy-related information in files created or edited by those programs.

SETTING BROWSER PRIVACY OPTIONS

You are able to control the amount of advertising that is displayed on your browser by adjusting the settings for accepting cookies or allowing popups. Below are detailed setup procedures for three browsers: Firefox version 2, Internet Explorer version 6, or Internet Explorer version 7. These procedures may not work for earlier or later versions of these browsers. If you have trouble carrying out these procedures, check the documentation or help files of your particular browser.

Setting Firefox Cookie Options

In Firefox, you can set up the browser to prompt you and ask you how you wish to treat each cookie:

1. From the Firefox menu bar, choose **Tools**.
2. Choose **Options...** from the pull-down menu to open the **Options** dialog box.
3. Select the **Privacy** tab.
4. In the **Cookies** section, make sure the **Accept cookies from sites** check box is checked.
5. In the **Keep until:** pull-down menu, choose the **ask me every time** option.
6. If there are certain sites that you trust or online services that only work when cookies are active, choose the **Exceptions...** option to the right of that check box and add those sites.
7. Select **OK** to close the **Options** dialog box.

If a new cookie seems at all suspicious, or if you do not want a particular web site's cookie to have any extra information about your visit, simply reject the cookie.

Deleting Cookies in Firefox

To delete cookies, do the following:

1. From the Firefox menu bar, choose **Tools**.
2. Choose **Options...** from the pull-down menu, which will open the **Options** dialog box.
3. Select the **Privacy** tab.
4. In the **Cookies** section, select **Show Cookies...** to open the **Cookies** dialog box.
5. To delete an individual cookie, select the cookie and then select the **Remove Cookies** option.
6. To delete all cookies, choose the **Remove All Cookie**s option.
7. Select **Close** to exit the **Cookies** dialog box.
8. Select **OK** to close the **Options** dialog box.

Blocking Popups in Firefox

To block popups, do the following:

1. From the Firefox menu bar, choose **Tools**.
2. Choose **Options...** from the pull-down menu to open the **Options** dialog box.
3. Select the **Content** tab.
4. Make sure the **Block pop-up Windows** check box has been checked.
5. Select **OK** to close the **Options** dialog box.

To allow popups on some sites, return to the **Content** tab of the **Options** dialog box, choose **Exceptions...** to the right of the **Block pop-up Windows** check box, and add the addresses of the allowed sites.

Setting Internet Explorer 6 Cookie Options

Internet Explorer allows you to set the types of cookies the browser will accept. To set up your browser:

1. Choose **Tools** from the menu bar.
2. Select **Internet Options...** from the pull-down menu to open the **Internet Options** dialog box.
3. Choose the **Privacy** tab.
4. Choose **Advanced...** to open up the **Advanced Privacy Settings** dialog box.
5. Choose the **Override automatic cookie handling** check box.
6. Choose an option under the **First-party Cookies** column and the **Third-party Cookies** column.
7. Select **OK** to close the **Advanced Privacy Settings** dialog box.

8. Select **OK** to close the **Internet Options** dialog box.

Deleting Cookies in Internet Explorer 6
To delete a cookie, or to see what cookies are on your computer, do the following:

1. Choose **Tools** from the menu bar.
2. Select **Internet Options...** from the pull-down menu to open the **Internet Options** dialog box.
3. Choose the **General** tab in the dialog box.
4. Choose the **Settings...** tab in the **Temporary Internet files** section to open the **Settings** dialog box.
5. Select **View files...** to see the list of files in the Windows Explorer file management program.
6. Choose and delete any cookie the same way you would delete a file.
7. Close Windows Explorer when done.
8. Select **OK** to close the **Settings** dialog box.
9. Select **OK** to close the **Internet Options** dialog box.

To delete all the cookies, after step three, choose the **General** tab and then choose **Delete Cookies...**, which will then give you the option of deleting all the cookies.

Blocking Popups in Internet Explorer 6
To block popups, do the following:

1. Choose **Tools** from the menu bar.
2. Select **Internet Options...** from the pull-down menu to open the **Internet Options** dialog box.

3. Choose the **Privacy** tab.
4. Make sure the **Block pop-ups** check box is checked.
5. To have a notification display when a popup is blocked, choose **Settings...** to open up the **Pop-up Blocker Settings** dialog box.
6. In the **Notifications and Filter Level** area of the dialog box, choose the desired **Filter Level** from the pull-down menu.
7. Select **Close** to exit the **Pop-up Blocker Settings** dialog box.
8. Select **OK** to close the **Internet Options** dialog box.

Setting Internet Explorer 7 Cookie Options

The procedure is quite similar to the one for Internet Explorer 6:

1. If the menu bar is not visible, right-click anywhere on the toolbar and select **Classic Menu** from the pull-down menu.
2. Choose **Tools** from the menu bar.
3. Select **Internet Options...** from the pull-down menu to open the **Internet Options - Security at Risk** dialog box.
4. Choose the **Privacy** tab.
5. Choose **Advanced...** to open up the **Advanced Privacy Settings** dialog box.
6. Choose the **Override automatic cookie handling** check box.
7. Choose an option under the **First-party Cookies** column and the **Third-party Cookies** column.

8. Select **OK** to close the **Advanced Privacy Settings** dialog box.
9. Select **OK** to close the **Internet Options – Security at Risk** dialog box.

Deleting Cookies in Internet Explorer 7
To delete cookies, do the following:

1. If the menu bar is not visible, right-click anywhere on the toolbar and select **Classic Menu** from the pull-down menu.
2. Choose **Tools** from the menu bar.
3. Select **Internet Options...** from the pull-down menu to open the **Internet Options** dialog box.
4. Choose the **General** tab.
5. In the **Browsing history** section, select **Settings** to open the **Temporary Internet Files and History Settings** dialog box.
6. Select **View trusted files** to see the list of files in the Windows Explorer file management program.
7. Choose and delete any cookie the same way you would delete a file.
8. Close Windows Explorer.
9. Select **OK** to close the **Temporary Internet Files and History Settings** dialog box.
10. Select **OK** to close the **Internet Options** dialog box.

Blocking Popups in Internet Explorer 7
To block popups, do the following:

1. If the menu bar is not visible, right-click anywhere on the toolbar and select **Classic Menu** from the pull-down menu.
2. Choose **Tools** from the menu bar.
3. Place your cursor over **Pop-up Blocker** from the pull-down menu.
4. If the popup blocker is off, select **Turn on Pop-up Blocker**.
5. If the popup blocker is on, select **Pop-up Blocker Settings...** to open the **Pop-up Blocker Settings** dialog box.
6. In the **Filter Level** section, choose the desired level of popup blocking from the pull-down menu.
7. Select **Close** to exit the **Pop-up Blocker Settings** dialog box.

PROTECT YOUR HOME WIRELESS NETWORK

Performing any of the following steps will help you maintain your privacy when using a wireless network, and performing all of the steps will help even more.

- **Change the router's user name and password**: Use something other than the default user name and password in order to make it harder for a hacker to access your system.
- **Control access with a user name and password**: Most wireless routers have a mechanism called identifier broadcasting. It sends out a service set identifier (SSID) signal or an extended service set identifier (ESSID) signal to any device in the vicinity announcing its presence. Change the default user name to a unique user name. For

added protection, set it up to require a password for access.
- **Turn off identifier broadcasting**: Hackers near your home can use identifier broadcasting to locate unprotected wireless networks. Disable this mechanism if your wireless router allows it.
- **Turn off wireless network when not in use**: If you will not be using your wireless network for an extended period of time, turn it off or disconnect it. Hackers are unable to gain unauthorized wireless access to your computers if the wireless network is not operating.
- **Use encryption**: The most effective way to secure your wireless network from intruders is to encrypt, or scramble, communications over the network. Typically, the default setting is to have this system turned off. Follow the directions included with your wireless router, or the product support information on the manufacturer's web site, to turn on encryption. Turning on encryption will allow access only to users with the proper user names and passwords. If your wireless router doesn't have an encryption feature, consider getting one that does. Two main types of encryption are available: Wired Equivalent Privacy (WEP) and the more secure Wi-Fi Protected Access (WPA). Your computer, router, and other equipment must use the same encryption.
- **Be careful away from home**: If you are accessing the Internet through a public hot spot, do not use this connection for anything involving sensitive private information.

Remove Privacy Data from Your Programs

Applications on your home computer may allow you to add personal information such as a name or address. Each time a file is created, that information becomes part of that file. For every program you use to create files that are then sent to others, make sure the programs are set up so no personal information becomes part of any newly created file.

Setting Up Windows and Outlook Express

The Windows operating system, as well as the Outlook Express email program that comes bundled with this operating system, has some features that will help protect your computer from viruses and other malicious software. Although not as full featured as dedicated privacy protection software, it would be a smart idea to make sure these features are active on your computer.

The suggestions that follow assume you are running some version of Windows XP that includes the updates that were a part of Service Pack 2, and that you also are running Internet Explorer version 6 or 7 and Outlook Express. If you are not running these versions of Windows XP and Outlook Express, check with your help files or other documentation. Also, if you haven't updated your Windows XP operating system to include either Service Pack 2 or the most recent security updates, you can do so using one of the following methods:

- Select **Tools** from the Internet Explorer the menu bar, and then select **Windows Update** from the pull-down menu.
- Visit http://windowsupdate.microsoft.com and follow the directions.

Activate the Windows XP Firewall

The Windows XP firewall offers limited protection against malicious software, usually much more limited than full-featured security software. If this will be the only firewall you use, be sure to follow the procedure below to activate the Windows XP firewall:

1. Select the Windows **Start** button, and then select **Control Panel** from the pull-down menu.
2. Once the new window opens, select **Security Center** to open the **Windows Security Center** dialog box.
3. If information within the dialog box shows that a firewall is on, simply close the dialog box.
4. If the dialog box shows that no firewall is active, follow the steps to enable the Windows firewall.

Use Windows XP Password Protection

Another way to protect the privacy of your family's computer is to give each family member his or her own protected area of the computer. Windows XP allows you to set up separate user accounts for each family member. A parent could also set up a child's area to prevent the child from reading any other user's files. To create or edit user accounts, do the following:

1. Select the Windows **Start** button, and then select **Control Panel** from the pull-down menu.
2. In the **Control Panel** window, select the **User Accounts** option to open the **User Accounts** dialog box.
3. From there, you can change an account or create an account.

4. Give the user an administrator account if you want that person to be able to add, change, or delete accounts; change passwords, install programs, and access all files. Otherwise, do not give that person an administrator account.

Review Outlook Express Signature Files

Most email programs, including Outlook Express, allow you to create a signature file that automatically adds a signature block to the end of any outgoing email. Be sure that you do not have any sensitive information in this signature file. For example, there is usually no need to add your full name, address, and telephone number on all outgoing emails. To see what may be in your signature block in Outlook Express, do the following:

1. Select the **Tools** option from the menu bar.
2. Select **Options…** from the pull-down list to open the **Options** dialog box.
3. Select the **Signatures** tab, and review the contents of any signatures that have been created. Remove any private information from the signature file.

Reviewing the Signature Files of Other Email Programs

If you use an email program other than Outlook Express, check the documentation or help files of that program to learn how to check the signature files.

STEP 3: ADD SOFTWARE TO PROTECT PRIVACY

The previous section discussed how to set up your operating system, browser, and email program to help protect your family's privacy. This section will describe how additional software can enhance that protection by addressing risks caused by malicious software.

DEALING WITH MALICIOUS SOFTWARE

Malicious software can enter your computer as a result of visiting a web site, from a file attached to an email, from a portable data storage device, or from a variety of other routes. There are three general types of software that can protect your computer by either preventing malicious software from loading on your computer, or by finding and removing malicious software that does make it to your computer:

- **Antispyware**: Software designed to detect or remove spyware, or to prevent spyware from being installed.
- **Antivirus**: Software designed to either prevent viruses from invading a computer, or to remove viruses already residing on a computer.
- **Firewall**: Software that controls communications between a personal computer and the Internet and prevents unauthorized access to that computer.

Malicious software represents a threat that continues to evolve. To keep ahead of this evolution, make sure your operating system, browser, and any additional protective software is updated regularly.

Virus Filtering in Outlook Express
Outlook Express can provide some protection from viruses that may be associated with incoming email. To ensure the program is set up to do this, do the following:

1. Choose **Tools** from the menu bar.
2. Choose **Options...** from the pull-down menu to open the **Options** dialog box.
3. Select the **Security** tab.
4. Look under the **Virus Protection** section and make sure the **Restricted sites zone** radio button is selected.
5. Make sure the check box next to **Do not allow attachments to be saved or opened that could potentially be a virus** is selected.
6. Select OK to close the **Options** dialog box.

Filter External Content in Outlook Express
Emails are commonly written in plain text or in HTML, which is a computer language used to control how a browser displays a web page. When you open an email formatted in HTML, it will behave like a web page and load images and other external content. This may be a privacy concern if the external content allows a malicious program to attack your computer. To open formatted emails without loading graphics or other external content, do the following:

1. Choose **Tools** from the menu bar.
2. Choose **Options...** from the pull-down menu to open the **Options** dialog box.
3. Select the **Security** tab.
4. Once the dialog box opens, look in the **Download Images** section to make sure the check box next to **Block images and other external content in HTML email** is checked.
5. Select OK to close the **Options** dialog box.

OTHER OPTIONS FOR PROTECTING YOUR COMPUTER
Appendix 1 lists a number of free software packages that can supplement the protection that is already built into Windows XP or Outlook Express. That appendix includes listings for programs to block, find, or eliminate viruses, spyware, and other threats to your computer. Appendix 2 has a number of free online privacy resources and privacy-related information. In addition to the resources in this book, you can also check the following resources:

- **Software vendors**: You may want to compare other options by reviewing consumer-oriented computer magazines or web sites that rate and compare software. Appendix 2 describes two such sites, Download.com and Sourceforge.net.
- **Your computer manufacturer**: If you are buying a new computer, check with the manufacturer to see if protective software is included with your purchase.
- **Your Internet service provider**: Check with your Internet service provider to see if antispyware, firewall, antivirus, or other protective software is offered with your service.

STEP 4: ADOPT HABITS THAT PROTECT PRIVACY
The earlier sections of this chapter dealt with developing a family privacy policy, making a home wireless system more secure, and either setting up or adding software to help maintain your family's privacy. These efforts would be wasted if your family does not practice good privacy habits. It is up to you and your child to avoid behavior that allows privacy-related information from escaping your family's control.

Good privacy habits are based on common sense. Parents have the responsibilities of providing guidance with respect to private and personal information, monitoring a child's habits, and making appropriate suggestions or changes. The following three habits should be a central part of any family's efforts to maintain online privacy:

1. Creating family privacy rules.
2. Managing user names and screen names.
3. Creating and managing passwords.

CREATING FAMILY PRIVACY RULES

In addition to having your child sign an Internet use agreement that has general rules about online behavior, you should also have rules for specific situations. The following suggestions cover several common privacy-related situations, and you may also add your own rules to cover other situations that may affect you or your child:

- **Joining mailing lists**: Your child should get your permission before signing up for any mailing list. A mailing list is a managed list of email addresses and other personal information that is used by an individual or organization when sending email. You should review the first few mailings to make sure the content is acceptable to you.
- **Responding to suspicious requests**: Teach your child not to respond to suspicious requests and to inform you when this kind of request arrives.
- **Sending or publishing personal information**: Your child should always first get your approval before putting any personal information online.

You should also minimize the amount of online personal information about your child.

- **Sending sensitive information**: An adult should be directly involved in this kind of transaction. Unless you are certain you can send data securely online, use a safe offline method like regular mail.
- **Signing up for online services**: Your child should get your permission before signing up for any online service that requires any information beyond a user name or password.
- **Using instant messaging (IM) or chat rooms**: The best kind of screen name for your child is one that gives no clues as to identity, location, age, or gender. In addition, your child should avoid including any personal or private information in an IM or a chat room conversation.
- **Visiting web sites**: Your child must first get your permission before sending any personal information to a web site.
- **Volunteering personal information**: Your child should never volunteer any personal information.
- **When in doubt, do nothing**: Instruct your child not to send any message or post anything online if there are any doubts about doing so.

MANAGING USER NAMES AND SCREEN NAMES

User names and screen names often represent the public face of a user's online activities. For example, for many online email accounts, the user name is the same as the portion of the email that comes before the "@" symbol. For services like IM, your child's screen name should be the only identification others should see, and it should be the only name your child uses if the conversation involves a stranger.

The one basic rule for user names and screen names is that they should contain no personal information such as name, age, gender, location, or affiliations. If your child's user name or screen name includes any identifying information about her, you or she should create a name that does not contain this type of information.

Your child will probably need user names or screen names for several online activities, and a sensible approach is to create a unique user name for each activity that uses private or sensitive information. Some examples include a Web-based email account, a school account, or a public library account. For an activity that has no sensitive data and that only requires a user name and password, it is safe to use the same user name in multiple places.

Remembering User Names and Screen Names

Keeping track of all the user names, screen names, and other information about every online service your child may use can be a nightmare. An easy way to manage all of this information together is to write it down and put it into the same notebook that has the family's Internet use agreements. You can use the "List of Online Activities" form that is included in the Family Forms Pack file located at http://forms.speedbrake.com.

CREATING AND MANAGING PASSWORDS

Passwords are an important tool for maintaining online privacy. It should not take a lot of time to create appropriate passwords or to keep track of them once they have been created.

How Strong Should a Password Be?

If a password is for an account that can be easily replaced and contains no sensitive information, the password can be something easy to remember. Otherwise, a strong password is appropriate.

Creating a Basic Password

A basic password has one or more of the following characteristics:

- All characters are either upper case or lower case.
- It can be found in a dictionary or reference book.
- It consists of a string of identical characters.
- It is the name of a person, place, or event.
- It is the same as the user name or screen name.

Although you can use the same basic password with several online accounts, you may want to create different basic passwords for each person in your family.

Creating a Strong Password

A strong password is one that would be very hard to guess, but very easy to create or to remember. One method for making a strong password is to take a word that is easy for you to remember, substitute some of the letters with numbers and special characters, and capitalize at least one letter. For example, take the word *parents*. With a few changes, it can become *p@R&nt$* or perhaps *p&r3N?z*.

Another method for creating a password that is even harder to guess is to take a favorite title, quotation, or line of poetry, write down the first letter of the first few words, and then use the second method on the resulting string of characters. For example, one of the most famous Shakespeare quotations, "To be, or not to be, that is the question," has ten words. The first letters from the first six words are *tbontb*. With a little imagination, you could take those six characters and turn them into something like *2B0#tb* or even *tbR@2b*.

Keeping Track of Passwords

You can keep track of passwords the same way you keep track of user names and screen names. Keeping them stored electronically may be an option, but it is a good idea to keep a copy of this information on paper as well. You can do this using the "List of Online Activities" in the Family Forms Pack at http://forms.speedbrake.com.

STEP 5: CREATE AND USE AN ONLINE ALIAS

One of the great advantages of the Internet is that you can participate in most online activities without revealing your identity. Some of those obvious exceptions would be transactions that require your legal name such as any dealings you may have with a bank, an airline, or your child's school.

Should You Use an Online Alias?

If you are legally obligated to provide true information about yourself, it would be wrong and possibly a crime to provide something other than true information. For just about any other online activity, if the service provider has no need to know your true identity, then do not provide it. If the answer to the next two questions is "no," feel free to use an online alias:

1. Are you legally required to provide information about yourself?
2. Would anyone suffer any kind of loss if you did not provide true personal information?

What Should Be in an Online Alias?

An online alias should consist of the kind of personal information that providers of online services typically ask of new users. If you can, leave as many of these fields blank as possible. If you have to enter some information, you may want to consider using some of these suggested alternatives:

- **Name**: A single letter or a string of random letters
- **Address**: 123 Main Street
- **City**: Beverly Hills
- **State**: CA (California)
- **Zip code**: 90210
- **Telephone**: 310-555-1234
- **Year of birth**: 1908
- **Income**: Pick something in the low range

My Life as a 99-year-old Woman

The example alias given above was not created out of thin air, but rather from my own experience. In all the times I have used some or all of this alias to register for various free online services, it was rejected only one time. The automated registration process of one online service recognized the street as not being one from Beverly Hills and was not satisfied until I provided an actual Beverly Hills street name.

Step 6: Respond Carefully to Requests

There are two kinds of online requests for personal information, the kind where there is a prior relationship with the requesting organization or individual and the kind where there is no prior relationship. For the first type of request, determine if the request is legitimate. If it is, respond using whatever communication method you typically use for that requester. If it is the second type of request, you should first determine if the request is legitimate. You also have to decide how to communicate private information reliably and securely. Typical options are communicating by regular mail, by phone, or by a secure web page.

It makes sense to be careful when responding, since a fraudulent request can be made to look like it came from a legitimate source. Recognizing the characteristics of a fraudulent request is the first step to protecting your family from a potential loss of privacy.

Characteristics of Fraudulent Requests

The messages that are more likely to be bogus are those that have one or more of the following characteristics:

- It contains a financial offer that is inappropriate to the recipient, for example a child receiving a credit card or mortgage refinancing offer.
- Something about the request makes you or your child feel uncomfortable.
- The message has several grammatical and spelling errors.
- The request appears to originate from a country where you and your child have no previous business or personal relationships.

- The request claims that personal information is needed to fix a problem.
- The request was contained in a popup.
- The subject line is blank, is in lowercase letters, is in an unfamiliar language, or doesn't make sense.
- There is an offer or promise of a high-value coupon or prize, or a significant amount of money in exchange for providing personal information.
- You are directed to visit a URL (a web site address) in order to provide personal information.
- You are requested to provide a password.
- You or your child are asked to provide sensitive personal information such as your full name, birth date, or Social Security number.

HOW TO CHECK IF A MESSAGE IS LEGITIMATE

Just because a request has fraudulent characteristics does not make it a fraudulent request. If you believe that it is a legitimate request, then your response will depend on the kind of request. The following are a few examples:

- **Email requests that ask you to visit a URL**: If an email appears to be from an organization or individual with a prior relationship to you, and asks that you to go to a particular URL, do not do so. Instead, contact the source directly to confirm that the request is legitimate. Do this using the same means you normally use to make contact.
- **Request made by a web site**: If you are asked to submit sensitive personal information through a web page, look at the URL. It should look like a legitimate URL. For example, if you think that the URL should end with *yourbank.com* and instead

ends with something else like *yourbank.xyz.com* or *yourbank.ru*, then you should not submit any information. The URL should also begin with *https://* rather than *http://*. Data sent from a page that has a URL that begins with *https://* is encrypted, so only the intended recipient should be able to read the data.
- **Request mentioning a problem with an account**: If the message appears to be from an organization where you have some kind of account, do use any of the addresses provided in the message. Instead, contact that organization in the way you normally do and check on the status of that account.

REQUESTS DIRECTED AT CHILDREN
Make it clear to your child that you should be informed any time she receives an online request for information, and should respond only if you have given approval. Your child should also tell you if she receives a request to contact someone by phone or to meet in person.

STEP 7: REVIEW YOUR FAMILY'S ACTIVITIES
No matter how many privacy rules you may have in place, your child may still have too much private and personal information available online. You can reduce your child's risks by regularly reviewing her online activities. You can use the "List of Online Activities" from the Family Forms Pack as a checklist, making note of any changes that should be made. A few examples of the things you may have to correct include the following:

- Having inappropriate people in an email address book or on a list of contacts in an online account.

- Not using a strong password on an account with sensitive information.
- Placing too much personal information about any family member in a web site.
- Placing too much personal information in the user profile section of any online service.
- Using passwords, user names, or screen names that contain personal information such as birth year, name, address, or gender.

Recognizing a Privacy Problem

Even if you implement all of the recommended actions in this chapter, you can still have privacy problems. The following is just a partial list of the kinds of things that could signal a privacy problem:

- A computer or any storage device with sensitive files is lost, stolen, or damaged.
- Files or programs are mysteriously missing, damaged, or altered.
- New software has been loaded on the computer without your approval.
- Sudden changes appear in your child's behavior or online activity.
- You discover that your child has placed sensitive personal information on a publicly accessible web page or web site.
- You discover that your child is providing personal data or photos to someone without your approval.
- You receive email or other communications from a person you do not know, and the messages indicate that the person knows quite a bit about you or your family.

TOP 10 PRIVACY PROTECTION TIPS

1. Make protecting privacy a regular part of your family's online habits.
2. Use your wireless network's security features.
3. Use your browser to control cookies and popups.
4. Use privacy protection software, including firewall, antivirus, and antispyware programs.
5. Regularly update your operating system and privacy protection software.
6. Keep a written record of every family member's passwords, user names, and other information needed to access any computer or online service.
7. Learn how to create passwords that are hard to guess, but easy to remember.
8. Do not volunteer personal information.
9. Use an online alias whenever it is appropriate.
10. Regularly review your family's online activities and address any potential security problems.

Chapter 5

Security Online

In This Chapter
- Key Security-related Threats
- Seven Steps to Online Security
- Recognizing a Security Problem
- Top 10 Security Protection Tips

Because going online is a normal, everyday activity for people from all walks of life, it should be no surprise that just as in the offline world, there is a small percentage of people online who are up to no good; trying to break into your computer, steal your money, or damage your data. Many online security threats can be avoided using a combination of savvy personal behavior and appropriate technology. As was the case with the privacy issues discussed in the previous chapter, the key to addressing security issues is to encourage behavior in your child that minimizes security risks, and that gets your child into the habit of staying safe online.

What Does Security Mean?

One useful definition of online security is the ability to identify, manage, or eliminate threats to information, to technology, or to the well-being of a group or individual.

For your family, those threats include attempts to steal, damage, or disable your home computer; attempts to steal the information in your computer or data storage device, and attempts to physically or psychologically harm your child.

Why Online Security Is Important

Identifying, reducing, or eliminating potential online threats to your child is important because of the potential consequences if those threats become real. Just as was the case with online privacy, a child who is new to the Internet and has not yet developed the judgment and skills to avoid dangerous situations is at the greatest risk. Some of the online security hazards your child may face include the following:

- Attempts by strangers to meet with a child.
- Attempts to destroy or steal information.
- Attempts to fraudulently obtain passwords, user names, or other security data.
- Online contacts with potential child predators.
- Unauthorized access to an online account.

Relationship of Privacy to Security

Internet security issues are often closely related to Internet privacy issues. Many potential online security problems begin as privacy problems and may later develop into security problems. For example, whenever someone has unauthorized access to a computer, there is a privacy problem because that person has access to all of the information on the computer. It is a potential security issue because any data on that computer can now be copied, changed, or destroyed. Privacy and security are also related because the tools, techniques, and habits that reduce or eliminate privacy threats can also reduce or eliminate many potential security threats.

EXAMPLES OF SECURITY-RELATED INFORMATION

The most valuable security-related information is any information that can give a criminal, child predator, or other undesirable person access to your personal data, to your computer, or to your child. Some of the items on the following list are also featured in chapter 4:

- Critical data in your computer, in your data storage devices, or in one of your online accounts.
- Current address or phone number.
- Lifestyle information such as travel schedules, group affiliations, clubs, favorite activities, and details about personal relationships.
- Salary, credit card information, bank account details, and other financial data.
- User names, passwords, or other data needed to access computers, computer networks, or online services.

EXAMPLES OF SECURITY-RELATED PROBLEMS

Most of security problems, even those that are hardware oriented, start with the actions of your child or of another family member.

- **Arranging to meet strangers**: This is a particularly worrisome security problem for families, since there are many predators who use the Internet to arrange meetings with potential victims.

- **Being careless with equipment**: Your child should know how to properly operate and care for any computer system in your home, especially basic tasks such as the proper procedures for turning the system on or shutting the system down.
- **High-risk online behavior**: There are some online activities; for example, using chat rooms and webcams, that attract the wrong kind of attention, especially if children are involved. According to the FBI, child predators often use these tools to evaluate their potential victims.
- **Not backing up data**: Any information that is on a hard drive may be lost or damaged for any number of reasons. Regularly backing up data is a very easy way to prevent this problem.
- **Responding to information requests**: This is the same kind of threat that was described in the privacy chapter. Fraudulent requests for passwords and other personal information may lead to a security problem, so you and your child should be aware of how to respond to these kinds of requests.

KEY SECURITY-RELATED THREATS

As was the case with risks to privacy, security risks can be divided into three broad categories: those that are caused by personal behavior, those that are caused by hardware or software, and those that are due to a combination of the first two categories. The following sections describe a variety security threats from these three categories.

Fraudulent Schemes

These are the same schemes that were described in the privacy chapter. It is a privacy issue if you lose control of your personal information. It becomes a security issue of that information is used against you or your child. For a detailed description of common fraudulent schemes and specific steps you and your family can take to address this class of online problems, please review chapter 4.

Hardware and Software Security Issues

Hardware-related security issues include all the privacy-related issues covered in the previous chapter, and they also include the challenges of controlling access to your family's data and making sure the data is not lost, damaged, or destroyed. Software issues are for the most part the same as what were described in chapter 4. There are some additional security concerns where software plays a role, and the following list provides a brief overview of those concerns:

- **File sharing software**: This class of software allows users to transfer files from one personal computer to another. If this software is on your computer, it could allow anyone on the Internet to access any file on your computer. You should keep this kind of software off your computer and remove it if already installed.
- **Hard drives and portable storage media**: Security may be compromised if personal data that is stored on a personal computer is stolen or if the computer is given away or sold with your family's personal data still on the hard drive. Also, you should take

steps to ensure that portable storage media such as CD-ROMs or flash drives are not lost or stolen.

- **Lost or stolen computers**: You can keep a lost or stolen computer from becoming a security disaster by making sure you have backup copies of key data and by keeping as little sensitive information on your family's computer as possible.

> **Laptop Security and Airline Travel**
> For years, airline travel with a laptop has meant exposing your computer to theft and damage every time you take it out for a security inspection. Your laptop is especially vulnerable if you are taken aside for additional screening and your laptop is out of your sight. Make it a habit to prepare your laptop before you fly. Erase any files with sensitive data. Copy the critical files that need to travel with you and keep them in a flash drive or other data storage device that is packed separately from your laptop's carrying case.

ONLINE HABITS THAT REDUCE RISK

Your child's online habits can directly affect the security risks that you and your family may face. Some of the habits that reduce risks include the following:

- **Backing up data**: There is an old saying in the computer industry that there are two kinds of users, those who have lost data and those who will. Losing data will happen, but if you and your child make backing up your files a regular habit, most of your data will always be safe.

- **Keeping track of software**: Having a process for deciding what software is added to your computer is one way to keep inappropriate or potentially malicious software from being installed.
- **Keeping track of data**: It is easy to keep track of data when it is stored on a computer. When you or your child store files in other places such as a flash drive or CD-ROM, you have to make the effort to keep track of the data or you will risk losing it.
- **Protecting computers and accessories**: Computers do not respond well to rough treatment. You have to make sure that everyone in the family understands how to take care of computers, printers, displays, and other devices and what to do to reduce the risks of accidental damage.
- **Verifying requests for information**: Your family should have a process for verifying that any request for information is a legitimate one.

SEVEN STEPS TO ONLINE SECURITY

Prevention is the best way to deal with security concerns. Many threats can be addressed using a combination of appropriate technology and sensible online behavior. The appropriate technology involves your personal computer hardware and software. Online behavior contributes to security by steering your family away from risky situations. The following general actions should help your family become more secure online:

1. Develop a family plan.
2. Set up your family's computer system to ensure its physical security.

3. Add software designed to protect your computer and computer data from unauthorized access.
4. Develop a process for managing the software on your computer.
5. Develop a process for regularly backing up data.
6. Develop a process for keeping track of data that is outside the computer.
7. Develop a process for regularly reviewing your family's online security efforts.

STEP 1: HAVE A FAMILY SECURITY PROTECTION PLAN

Chapter 2 discusses using a formal Internet use agreement with your child to outline how an agreement forms the foundation of your child's relationship with the Internet. If you allow your child to be online alone, the following should be included in the agreement:

- I will not install any software on any computer without getting my parents' permission.
- I will not open any file sent to me unless I get my parents' permission.
- I will allow my parents to access any account or look at any of my data any time they ask.
- I will not meet or agree to meet in person anyone I have only met online unless I have my parents' permission.
- I will be careful when I use the family's computer equipment.
- I will not let someone else use any of the family's computer equipment, without first getting my parent's permission.

STEP 2: SET UP YOUR HARDWARE

Hardware security is mostly basic physical security. The following suggestions will take care of most potential threats to your hardware:

- **Electrical issues**: Use a surge suppressor for your computer system. This device protects electronic devices from unexpected changes in voltage. These surges may be caused by appliances in the home being turned on or off, or from problems in the local power grid.
- **Food and drink**: Eating or drinking in the area around the computer is never a good idea.
- **Hardware setup**: Make sure the computer, printer, and other components are set up so they are not a trip hazard and will not be bumped or hit during routine household activities.

DISPOSING OF OLD COMPUTERS

The hard drive on your old computer probably contains thousands of files of every description. While you could erase the files, there is no guarantee that you will get rid of all of the data. There are options for disposing of a computer that will give you more control over your older data:

- **Destroy the hard drive**: If the computer can no longer be used, carefully take out the hard drive and damage it to the point that it can no longer be read. Keep in mind that a computer contains hazardous materials, and in most communities you must follow special procedures to dispose of computers and computer components.

- **Give it to a child**: If your child has developed the maturity and judgment needed to be online alone, let her use the computer to work online. If not, then only allow her to use the computer offline.
- **Use it offline**: Find useful tasks that the computer can do offline, freeing up your other computer for work that can only be done online.
- **Keep the computer**: If you can find no other use for the computer, keep it as a backup.

STEP 3: ADDING SOFTWARE PROTECTION

The protective software discussed in chapter 4 is also effective for preventing security issues caused by malicious software.

STEP 4: MANAGE THE SOFTWARE ON THE COMPUTER

Once you have a computer in your home, you or your child will want to add software to enhance the computer's capability and improve your online experience. A useful software management process has to have, at minimum, the following parts:

- **Approval process**: Parents should be responsible for deciding if a program should be added to or removed from the computer.
- **Evaluation process**: Before allowing new software on the family computer, find out if there have been any serious issues with the software. Web sites that evaluate software are described in the "Computer and Internet Resources" section of appendix 2.
- **Record-keeping process**: In Windows XP you can check to see what software is on your computer by choosing **Start> Control Panel> Add or Remove**

Programs. You can also have that information written down. When a new program goes on the computer, keep track of it using "List of Additional Software" form and put that form into the same notebook that has your family's Internet use agreements. You can find and download this by visiting http://forms.speedbrake.com.

STEP 5: HAVE A DATA BACKUP PROCESS
Regularly backing up your data, which involves making a copy of your important files and storing that copy separate from the computer, is probably the single most important thing that you can do to protect your data. You can always replace your hardware and software, but it may be impossible to replace data once it has been lost, stolen, or destroyed. Like exercising, the process is not too complicated, but getting into a regular habit can be an ongoing challenge. The following suggestions should make it easier:

- **Choose a family data manager**: This person should make sure all data is backed up and stored in a safe place.
- **Decide on data storage technology**: There are several hardware choices for storing backed-up data, including external hard drives, flash drives, DVD-ROMs, and CD-ROMs.
- **Schedule a regular backup time**: If you are not sure how often to back up data, do it monthly.

STEP 6: USE A DATA TRACKING PROCESS
Once your family is in the habit of regularly backing up data, everyone must be able to keep track of where all the

data resides. The person who is serving as the family data manager should also be responsible for this.

- **Keep a written record**: Use the "List of Data Storage Devices" that is part of the Family Forms Pack to keep track of where data is stored outside of your computer's hard drive.
- **Have a plan for securing sensitive data**: Sensitive data, such as medical records or financial records, should have a higher level of security than other files. The family data manager should decide if this data needs to have extra security, such as being kept in a locked file cabinet or even being stored outside of the home.

STEP 7: REGULARLY REVIEW ONLINE ACTIVITIES

Any review of your family's online security situation should include the seven-step privacy protection process described in chapter 4, as well as the following two activities:

1. Confirm the location of all the items listed in the "List of Data Storage Devices." Update the list to reflect any additions or changes.
2. Using the "List of Additional Software," make sure all the programs on your computer were approved by you. Remove any program that was not approved by you, or that no longer serves any useful purpose.

RECOGNIZING A SECURITY PROBLEM

Following the recommendations in this chapter is no guarantee that you and your family will be free of any security problems. Early signs of a security problem typically include activity or behavior that seems unusual, unexpected, or inappropriate. If you observe any of the following situations, you should take prompt action:

- Files or programs on your computer are mysteriously missing, damaged, or updated.
- A family member has unexplained or unusual financial activity in a bank account or credit card.
- A stranger attempts to arrange a meeting with your child.
- New or unfamiliar software is mysteriously loaded on your computer.
- Your computer has been affected by a virus or other malicious software.
- Your child is installing new software without your knowledge or permission.
- Your computer or any storage device with sensitive files is lost, stolen, or damaged.
- Your computer starts to behave strangely.

TOP 10 SECURITY PROTECTION TIPS

1. Make online and offline security a key part of your family's online habits.
2. Choose a family data manager who will track where the family's data is stored.
3. Back up data regularly.
4. Keep a written record of where data is stored.
5. Update your operating system software regularly.
6. Use security protection software programs and update them regularly.
7. Use software from reputable and reliable sources.

8. Take action if your computer starts to behave strangely.
9. Regularly review your family's online activities and address any potential security problems.
10. Either keep or destroy old hard drives.

Check out the *Parenting and the Internet* Podcast

If you would like to have to opportunity to listen to some of the highlights of the book, or hear me talk about ongoing changes in the Internet that affect the parents of online children, be sure to check out the podcast *Parenting and the Internet,* available online at http://podcast.speedbrake.com.

Chapter 6

Internet Legal and Ethical Issues

In This Chapter
- Copyrights and Trademarks
- Pornography and Free Speech
- Defamation and Libel Online
- Ten Tips for Avoiding Online Defamation
- Online Piracy

Two things are true about the Internet. The first is that there are tremendous resources available for anyone to use and enjoy, and the second is that there are rules about how you and your child can use those resources. If these rules are not followed, there could be trouble with your child's school, with your ISP, or even with someone's lawyer.

This chapter will review some of the most important legal issues that you and your child may face when using the information and services available online. Knowing some basic things about these issues will help you make decisions that will keep anyone in your family from doing things that can cause problems.

> Please note that this chapter, and for that matter the rest of the book, is not designed to provide any legal or professional advice. For further assistance on legal or other issues mentioned herein, please seek the services of a competent professional.

COPYRIGHTS AND TRADEMARKS

Copyrights and trademarks are forms of intellectual property protection that allow the owners to control how protected material can be used. The following are the basic facts that you and your child should know:

- Copyrights can apply to written works, sound recordings, and visual works.
- If something is freely available online, your child does not need any permission to read it, view it, or listen to it.
- If your child wants to publish copyrighted or trademarked material in a web page or web site, then she would have to get permission to do so.
- Most of the information published online is also copyrighted.
- The owner of a copyright can control how a work can be used, copied, altered, or distributed.
- Trademarks can apply to the words, symbols, or designs that identify a product. A closely related concept, the service mark, applies to a service rather than a product.

THE MOST IMPORTANT COPYRIGHTED MATERIAL

The copyrighted online material that should be of greatest concern to you is content that is protected by copyright and that your child may want to use in a web site, web page, or other online publication. Copyright owners of the following kinds of materials typically have restrictions about how their materials may be used and may take legal action if their content is used without permission:

- Books, newspapers, and magazines
- Music
- Videos

While it would be a violation to transmit or republish copyrighted material without permission, it is acceptable to provide readers with the URL of a copyrighted work.

ONLINE MATERIALS THAT ARE NOT PROTECTED

The following categories of material are not restricted and your child is free to use them in any way without getting anyone's permission:

- **Facts and ideas**: The words, drawings, or pictures used to express facts and ideas can be copyrighted, but not the underlying ideas or facts.
- **Government documents**: In the United States, almost anything published by local, state, or federal governments or their employees, including reports, films, and speeches, can be freely used.
- **Material in the public domain**: This is intellectual property that has had its protection expire, could not meet requirements for protection, or was never protected before being released to the public.
- **Older works**: In general, if the copyright holder of the work is a person who has been dead for more than 100 years, the work is in the public domain.

- **Titles, words, slogans, and phrases**: These items are not protected by copyright, so you are free to use them. However, if a trademark or service mark is associated with a title, word, slogan, or phrase, you may have some limitations.

FAIR USE AND COPYRIGHTED MATERIAL

One of the most important aspects of copyright for your child to understand is the principle of fair use. This is the legal use of copyrighted material without the permission of the copyright holder. The principle of fair use allows your child to do the following with copyrighted material he may find online:

- Print or save a document for personal use.
- Read, view, or listen to material online.
- Use material for educational purposes.

This last example of fair use is the most important one for your child because it allows him to use protected material without charge if it is connected with schoolwork or research.

Q&A ABOUT COPYRIGHT ISSUES

If it is already on the Internet, why can't I use it any way that I want?
Unless you know the material is in the public domain or has an expired copyright, assume that it is copyright protected. The copyright owner has the freedom to place a work online and to allow the public to view the work. To do almost anything else, you need to get permission.

Can I use someone's music on my web site to help attract visitors or to help raise money for charity?
Even if you are not making money from it or using it to raise money for charity, you still have to get permission to use a copyrighted work on your web site.

How do I know if something is copyrighted?
The easy way is to look for a copyright notice. A common way to indicate copyright is to use a combination of a copyright symbol, the year the work was first published, and the name of the copyright owner. For example, the copyright notice "Copyright © 2007 by Todd Curtis" is used in this book, but either "© 2007 Todd Curtis," or "Copyright 2007 Todd Curtis" would also be valid.

What if I don't see any copyright notice?
The work may still be protected by copyright since the notice is not required to be visible. If you want to republish part or all of that work, find the group or person who owns or controls the copyright and get permission to use it.

What if I find that my work is being used on a web site without my permission?
If you control the copyright to that work, and if it is being used in a way that you think does not meet the standards of fair use, you may want to request that it be removed. If the organization or person who is using your copyrighted work refuses, you can inform the company or ISP hosting that page that the use of the work is a copyright violation and request that the item be removed from the web site.

Can I put one of Shakespeare's plays on my web site?
You can place part or all of any of Shakespeare's words on your site because his work, like the work of most writers who have been dead for more than a century, is in the public domain.

Can I take a song from my music collection and use it on my web page?
In most cases, you would need to get permission. When you buy music, you have the right to listen to it, but not to republish it online unless the recording is in the public domain (rare for modern recordings) or if you have permission from the copyright holder.

What if I just sample few seconds of a song on my site?
It does not matter if it is just a few seconds. You would still need permission to use that copyrighted work.

Why can't I find newer books on the Web?
Most books that have been published in the last 100 years are still protected by copyright. For books published in the United States after 1977, the copyright expires 70 years after the death of the last surviving author.

Do I need to get permission or pay someone to use something from a web site for a school assignment?
No. The principle of fair use lets you use almost anything you want in a school assignment without first asking the copyright or trademark owner for permission. However, when you use someone else's work in your school project, you should clearly indicate the source of the information; for example, the URL.

What about using some old NASA videos in a video that I want to put online?
That would not be a problem. Most everything that is produced by a local, regional, state, or federal government organization in the United States is in the public domain. You can do whatever you want with it, even make money from it, and you do not have to obtain permission or pay anyone. Check with the government organization in question for any exceptions to these public domain rules.

How can I use selections from this book?
If you own a copy of my book, you are free to give it away or sell it to someone else. You can also use your own words to express any of the facts or ideas in this book and create a web site, magazine article, or even a new book. If you want to do something that does not meet the standards for fair use, you will need my permission, as the copyright owner.

PORNOGRAPHY AND FREE SPEECH

The Internet was largely a creation of the government of the United States and the laws and traditions of the United States have heavily influenced the extent of information that your child can find online. The Constitution of the United States, specifically the First Amendment, states:

> Congress shall make no law respecting an establishment of religion, or prohibiting the free exercise thereof; or abridging the freedom of speech, or of the press; or the right of the people peaceably to assemble, and to petition the Government for a redress of grievances.

The First Amendment forms the basis of laws and traditions in the United States that are related to both online and traditional publishing. The most important tradition for online publishing is freedom of speech, which is the right to express opinions, information, or ideas in public or in private, regardless of content, without interference by a government. This free speech tradition includes allowing adults to view or transmit sexually oriented material on the Internet.

WHAT IS PORNOGRAPHY?

Pornography is any material that is sexually explicit and that is intended to cause sexual arousal. Such material does not have to involve descriptions or depictions of nudity or sexual activity. In the United States, most forms of sexually explicit material are protected by the First Amendment, making it legal for adults to create, publish, or consume such material.

PORNOGRAPHY AND OBSCENITY

Pornographic material is different from obscene material. Obscene material has been legally determined to be sexually explicit, offensive to conventional standards of decency, and lacking in serious literary, scientific, artistic, or political value. It also does not have First Amendment protection, so it is illegal for anyone in the United States to view, possess, publish, or transmit such material.

PORNOGRAPHY AND CHILD PORNOGRAPHY

Like material that is considered to be obscene, material that is considered to be child pornography is illegal for anyone in the United States to view, possess, or publish. Child pornography is any kind of visual depiction of a person under the age of 18 engaged in sexually explicit conduct. The conduct does not have to involve either sexual acts or nudity.

ACCIDENTAL EXPOSURE TO PORNOGRAPHY
It is unlikely that your child will ever be accidentally exposed to obscene material or child pornography. Law enforcement organizations and Internet service providers are very aggressive about keeping these kinds of materials off the Internet. Unfortunately, most sexually explicit material is quite legal, and widely available online. What follows are a few examples of how your child may be accidentally exposed to this kind of content:

- **Your child is sent an email containing sexually explicit images**: In the United States, if the sender did not know that the recipient was under the age of 18, then the sender likely did not violate any federal or state laws. Internet service providers may have stricter limitations on what kind of behavior is allowed. You may want to report the incident to your ISP to see what actions can be taken.
- **Your child is sent a written message that contains sexually explicit language**: In the United States, sexually explicit writing has fewer restrictions than sexually explicit images. Unless there was some attempt to sexually solicit a child, it is likely that no law was broken. However, it may be worthwhile to at least report the incident to a service provider.
- **A child follows a link to an adult web site**: So long as the material has not been declared legally

obscene or does not involve child pornography, it is likely that no laws were broken.

> A link is a coded part of a web page that when selected takes a browser to some other online resource. A link may appear as highlighted, colored, or underlined text, or as part of another element of a web page, such as a picture, logo, or some other graphical element.

FREE SPEECH AND CHILDREN

As a parent, you are free to allow your child to have as much or as little free expression online as you want. Sensible restrictions include limits on the following:

- The kind of web sites that your child can visit.
- The kinds of videos your child may view.
- The language or vocabulary your child can use while online.
- The music, games, and other online entertainment options your child is allowed to enjoy.

Q&A ABOUT PORNOGRAPHY AND FREE SPEECH

Why can't I say anything I want online?
No country on earth, even countries with a long tradition of free speech, is without rules when it comes to what one can say or write. Beyond the laws that governments may enforce, ISPs and parents will also have rules about what is or what is not allowed online.

Do children have the same free speech rights as adults?
No. Children can have many more restrictions on their free speech rights than adults. Parents are allowed to provide as little or as much freedom of speech as they want. In the United States, both schools and libraries that accept federal funding for their online activities are required to restrict what children can do online.

Can I keep pornographic email from being sent to me?
Unfortunately, anyone with an email address can be sent unsolicited messages, including those containing adult-oriented material. Chapter 4 on privacy and chapter 9 on unwanted email have many suggestions for keeping such email to a minimum, but there is no way to completely eliminate the problem.

DEFAMATION AND LIBEL ONLINE

Defamation is a legal term for a false statement that causes harm to someone's reputation, or that causes that person to become a target of public contempt, hatred, ridicule, or condemnation. Libel is defamation that is either written or broadcast.

HOW THIS MAY BECOME A PROBLEM

Participating in rumors or gossip about the actions or behaviors of others is a normal occurrence among adults and children. When people talk to one another, the target of the conversation may be spoken of disparagingly, but there is usually nothing left behind to connect a false statement with any particular person. When that kind of statement is sent to others online, however, it can be very easy to connect a message with its sender, which could lead to the following kinds of problems:

- If your ISP gets complaints about messages that were sent from your account, then the ISP may suspend or cancel your service.
- Students who make or pass on false statements about other students or about staff members will likely face disciplinary actions such as loss of Internet privileges or suspension.
- The persons whose reputations are damaged by information sent or posted online may retaliate by bringing legal action.

TEN TIPS FOR AVOIDING ONLINE DEFAMATION

1. Assume that any message you or your child sends or publishes online will always be available.
2. Avoid sending jokes by email, especially if they are about a particular individual.
3. If someone sends or publishes something online about your child that is both untrue and upsetting, encourage your child to talk about it.
4. If you know the source of a message containing false statements about anyone in your family, make the ISP aware of the situation.
5. Avoid composing email while upset.
6. Don't email or publish embarrassing photos of anyone.
7. Avoid arguments and confrontations online.
8. Don't create or spread rumors or gossip online.
9. If your child discovers someone has used the Internet to spread rumors or lies about someone else, encourage your child to tell you about it.
10. If you have the slightest doubt about something you are about to do, then don't do it.

ONLINE PIRACY

Unlike centuries past, where piracy on the high seas was difficult and dangerous, online piracy is very easy. All it takes is the ability to copy or save a file. Quite simply, piracy is a kind of theft. It is the illegal or unauthorized copying, use, installation, or distribution of intellectual property such as software, videos, and music files. Your child does not have to go online to make an unauthorized copy of a file, but doing so online is more likely to lead to problems because it is more likely that your ISP or the owner of the pirated property will notice.

ONLINE PIRACY CAN LEAD TO LAWSUITS

The types of piracy most likely to cause problems for your child or for your family are the kinds where there is either a perceived or actual financial loss and the affected organization is willing to take action.

One of the most well-known examples of individual users being sued for acts of online piracy began in 2003 when the Recording Industry Association of America (RIAA), an organization representing the US recording industry, began suing thousands of people for allegedly using file sharing programs to download music illegally. Many settled out of court, sometimes paying thousands of dollars to avoid going to trial.

While this is an extreme case, it shows the potential problems that can happen when you allow someone in the family to download or copy files without permission. As is the case with privacy and security issues, having good online habits will help your family avoid many potential privacy problems.

Dealing with a Piracy at Home

Dealing with piracy in your home is a three-step process:

1. Do not allow your child to download or copy a pirated program or file either at home or away from home.
2. Have a process for adding any files or software to your family's computers.
3. Uninstall any program and erase any file you find that was not legally acquired.

Options to Piracy

Rather than simply saying no to piracy, you can talk with your child in order to find out why she wants a particular program or file. Perhaps you will find a satisfactory compromise, or perhaps you will decide she will not get that file or program. Either way, this kind of discussion leads to a more responsible use of the Internet by your child. Some options to piracy include the following:

- Purchasing the item from a legitimate source.
- Finding a free alternative to the desired item.
- Including the purchase of music or software in the regular family budget.

Chapter 7

Cyberbullies and Child Predators

In This Chapter
- Online Bullying
- Cyberbullying Warning Signs
- Top 10 Ways to Prevent Cyberbullying
- Child Predators and the Internet
- Law Enforcement Involvement
- Top 10 Tips for Avoiding Online Predators

There are several ways that your child can be harassed online, but the kinds of harassment that concern most parents are the kinds that could lead to psychological or physical harm. The two most likely sources of this kind of harm are cyberbullies and online child predators. Both kinds of harassers can be dealt with using some of the same approaches discussed in the chapters on privacy and security threats, and you can also fight these threats using the resources of your ISP, of your child's school, or of law enforcement.

Online Bullying

School bullying existed long before the creation of the Internet. The objective of an online bully is no different than the objectives of a traditional bully; it is generally to make the victim feel intimidated or threatened. Online bullying is psychological rather than physical, and could range from activities such as gossiping and teasing, to more serious actions such as sexual, religious, or racial harassment.

DEFINITION OF A CYBERBULLY
A person who is a cyberbully engages in repeated or coordinated cruel or harassing actions directed at an individual by means of email, IM, text message, blogs, web sites, or other online resources.

WHY IS CYBERBULLYING AN IMPORTANT ISSUE?
Parents should be concerned with this kind of harassment because it could have serious psychological effects on your child, and because threatening online behavior could escalate into more serious offline threats.

Learning to recognize cyberbullying behavior can help to protect your child from being a victim and can help you recognize if your child is becoming a perpetrator.

EXAMPLES OF CYBERBULLYING
Online bullying can take many forms, such as some of the following examples:

- Creating a web site or other online publication that makes a person an object of ridicule.
- Damaging, destroying, or altering someone's data, files, programs, or online publications.
- Making threats by using email, newsgroups, or some other online communication.
- Posting embarrassing photos of someone.

- Publicizing confidential personal information.
- Retaliating for other acts of bullying.
- Sending messages that are meant to be hurtful.
- Spreading rumors or gossip.

CYBERBULLYING ROLES

As with old-fashioned bullying, there are three ways in which your child may be involved in cyberbullying:

- As a victim
- As a perpetrator
- As a witness

While each kind of involvement may have different effects on your child, as a parent you have to be willing to take appropriate action whenever you recognize a potential problem.

CYBERBULLYING WARNING SIGNS

The early signs of cyberbullying are similar to the early signs of other online problems. Before jumping to conclusions, take the time to talk to your child and discover what may be happening. The following are some of the common warning signs:

- Avoiding friends or classmates.
- Significant change in mood.
- Spending much more or much less time online.
- Sudden changes in online or offline behavior.
- Your find out that your child is either sending or receiving threatening or harassing messages.
- You find out that your child or someone your child knows is being bullied online.

Responding to Cyberbullying

Unlike with threats to privacy and security, there is little you can do either through technology or personal online behavior to prevent your child from becoming a victim. However, there is plenty you can do to respond to an act of bullying.

1. **Talk to your child**: If you suspect there may be a problem, or if your child informs you about a cyberbullying situation, find out what you can about the situation, such as how long it has been occurring, and how the bullying took place.
2. **Gather and save relevant information**: Save copies of emails, web pages, or anything else proving that online bullying had taken place.
3. **Identify the source of the problem**: If you can, identify the source of the cyberbullying, such as email addresses and web site addresses. Also, ask your child if he knows who is responsible.
4. **Contact the appropriate organizations**: At the very least, you should contact any organization associated with the source of the cyberbullying, such as the service provider behind an email or a web page, or your child's school if a harassing message was sent from or to an account at the school.
5. **Take action**: You can do things such as asking an online service provider to remove a web page or block an email account. If appropriate, you may wish to contact your child's school and request that disciplinary action be taken.

Internet Use Agreement and Cyberbullying

If you allow your child to go online alone, you should include the following in the Internet use agreement:

- I will not use the Internet to bully anyone or to embarrass anyone.

Eliminating Bullying Behavior

Becoming a cyberbully is often not the result of one or two actions, but the result many small actions that may not seem significant at the time. For example, if your child makes fun of a classmate in an email and sends it to a second classmate, it represents a case of bad manners. If that second classmate sends copies of that message to the entire class, your child would be considered a cyberbully.

One of the best things you can do for your child is to encourage responsible online behavior, especially when it comes to talking about other people. A good start in that direction would be making sure your child follows the suggestions in the next section.

Top 10 Ways to Prevent Cyberbullying

1. Don't encourage anyone to use the Internet to bully someone.
2. If you can't say something nice about someone in an email, IM, chat room, or anywhere else on the Internet, then don't say it at all.
3. Don't email or publish online any embarrassing photographs, videos, or audio recordings.
4. If you know that someone is being bullied online, tell someone.

5. Don't send emails or other online messages that threaten a person.
6. Don't send emails or other online messages that use foul or abusive language.
7. Don't send or post angry messages online.
8. Follow family rules about online behavior.
9. Follow school rules about online behavior.
10. If you receive a threatening or harassing message, tell someone, especially a teacher or parent.

CHILD PREDATORS AND THE INTERNET

Adults who harm children have been around long before the Internet was invented. However, the Internet allows a predator to be a threat to the girl next door, or to the boy on the other side of the continent. Predator behavior has not changed, but their methods have changed to adapt to the technology of the Internet.

Child predators are a real and potentially devastating threat, but there are many things you can do to reduce the risk to your family. Ample resources, including those of law enforcement, are also available to help parents deal with the potential threats.

DEFINITION OF A CHILD PREDATOR

A child predator is any adult who actively works to develop a personal relationship with a child in order to cause some future harm. This harm can come either from an inappropriate or illegal online or offline relationship.

While the greatest fear in the hearts of parents is from a predator who wants to physically meet a child in order to cause physical harm, your child may also suffer serious psychological harm from a purely online relationship.

Chapter 7—Cyberbullies and Child Predators 109

WHY IS THIS ISSUE IMPORTANT?
Online child predators are an important issue for you because the threat exists any time your child is online. It is also important because as a parent, you are in the best position to recognize the symptoms of predatory online behavior and to take action to protect your child.

INITIAL CHILD PREDATOR BEHAVIOR
Most child predators go through a process called *grooming* where the predator works over a period of time to gain the trust of a potential victim by first building a relationship using online communication tools such as email, chat rooms, and instant messaging. Early contacts with a child may not be at all suspicious, and it may take several contacts by email, IM, or other communication before the predator exhibits inappropriate behavior. The early warning signs may include one or more of the following:

- Arranging to make contact with your child either by phone or in person.
- Asking your child to keep a conversation or an online relationship a secret.
- Providing your child with some kind of online account in order to have private conversations.
- Requesting personal information from your child such as age, address, or school information.
- Requesting that a child send a picture.
- Sending your child letters, photographs, or gifts.

Your child should be discouraged from having these kinds of contacts, accepting gifts from strangers, or giving out private information, even though there is nothing illegal about these actions.

ADVANCED CHILD PREDATOR BEHAVIOR
If any one of the following situations occurs, it could indicate that a child predator is pursuing your child and that a crime may have already occurred:

- **You discover your child engages in sexually explicit online conversations**: You should put a stop to any such conversations, and if you suspect an adult was involved, the appropriate authorities should be contacted.
- **You find pornography or other sexually explicit material on a computer your child uses, or on one of your child's portable data storage devices**: Often predators provide pornography to potential victims as a means of starting sexually oriented discussions. If you believe that an adult sent the material to your child, contact the authorities and provide them with copies of any files.
- **Your child receives phone calls from someone you don't know or the child is making calls, especially long distance ones, to numbers you don't recognize**: You should put a stop to these kinds of calls, and find out as much as possible about the numbers called, the time and date of calls, and duration of calls. Your monthly billing statement may include these kinds of details.
- **Your child calls someone known only through online contacts**: Potential child predators may provide contact numbers to your child, or may

even provide a toll-free number or tell your child to call collect.
- **Your child arranges to meet someone that he or she knows only from the Internet**: You should always be involved in any first-time meeting with anyone your child has met only online. A huge warning sign would be if the meeting involves any kind of travel. If you find out one day that your child has bus, train, or plane tickets to another city, or that your child expects a visitor from out of town, it is time for a serious talk.
- **Your child turns the computer or the display off, changes the screen, or closes an application when you enter the room**: If you see this happening, ask your child for an explanation and then review any recent activity on the computer.
- **Your child becomes withdrawn from friends, family, or normal activities**: Online predators sometimes work very hard at driving a wedge between children and their normal relationships. Children may also become withdrawn after sexual victimization or after having been exposed to disturbing information online.

CHILD PREDATOR PREVENTIVE ACTIONS

It is difficult to use technology to block child predators because predators may use several online and offline methods of communication. Predators often seek to gain the trust of potential victims by building a relationship, a relationship that could take weeks or months to develop. Your most effective prevention method is to take the time to be involved with your child's online activities and to be on the lookout for suspicious activity. The following suggestions should help you keep your child from encountering problems from predators:

- **Prohibit or closely supervise visits to chat rooms**: The Federal Bureau of Investigation (FBI) has found that most children who fall victim to online sexual predators spend large amounts of time online, particularly in chat rooms. Monitoring chat room activity means being with your child when she is in a chat room, or setting up your computer so all of her conversations can be reviewed later.
- **Prohibit or closely supervise a child's use of IM**: Instant messaging shares many of the risks associated with a chat room, and should have similar restrictions.
- **Closely supervise online contacts with strangers**: Whenever you find out that your child has any kind of ongoing communication with someone, talk to her and find out what the conversations are about. If the conversations or messages seem at all inappropriate, take steps to keep that person from contacting your child.
- **Do not allow your child to arrange a phone call or a meeting with someone known only from online contacts**: An adult should make the first contact with strangers. For added security, phone calls should be made or received at a phone other than your home phone, and any face-to-face meeting should occur in a public place with many potential witnesses.
- **Prohibit your child from sending personal photos to anyone without your permission**: This is a privacy issue and a child predator issue. Once a

photo is sent out, you lose control over how that image may be used. Exchanging photos is part of the grooming process of many child predators and may escalate from normal photos to those that are highly inappropriate.
- **Prohibit or closely supervise a child's use of a webcam**: A common tactic of online predators is to get the child to perform in front of a webcam. If someone only known to your child from online contacts either encourages your child to use an available webcam or sends one as a gift, this should be considered a huge warning sign.
- **Ensure that your child limits the amount of personal information shared online**: If you find that your child is giving personal information to strangers, make sure that she stops that behavior.
- **Prohibit or closely supervise late night online activity**: According to the FBI, children are at the greatest risk from online predators during the evening. While offenders are online around the clock, most work during the day and spend their evenings online trying to locate and lure children.

LAW ENFORCEMENT INVOLVEMENT

Should one or more of the following situations occur, immediately contact either a local or state law enforcement agency, or the local office of the FBI. The nonprofit National Center for Missing and Exploited Children has an online reporting service through the CyberTipLine at http://www.cybertipline.com:

- **Your child or anyone in the household has received child pornography**: Child pornography is

any kind of visual depiction of a person under the age of 18 engaged in sexually explicit conduct. The conduct does not have to involve either sexual acts or nudity.
- **Someone who knows your child is under the age of 18 sexually solicits your child**: This includes any situation where an adult makes a request to engage in sexual activity, has sexually oriented conversations, or makes requests for sexually oriented information.
- **Someone who knows your child is under the age of 18 sends your child sexually explicit images**: Sexually explicit images include images that show actual or simulated sexual activity, or images that exhibit the genitals or pubic area in a lewd or provocative way.
- **You find out that an adult has traveled or is planning to travel for the purpose of having sex with a minor:** In the United States, the FBI is particularly interested in cases involving traveling sexual predators. It does not matter if this person was planning to meet your child or planning to meet another child.

If any of the above situations occur, log out of any online service you are using and shut the computer down to preserve any evidence for future law enforcement use. Unless directed to do so by a law enforcement agency, do not attempt to copy any of the images or the text found on the computer. If the event involved an online service such as an email account, avoid using that service again until law enforcement has had a chance to review any activity.

THE FBI INNOCENT IMAGES INITIATIVE

The FBI has enlisted the help of dozens of local, state, and national law enforcement organizations to combat online child pornography and child exploitation. Starting in 1995, the Innocent Images Initiative has targeted web sites, individuals, and organizations involved in the criminal exploitation of children.

Since 2004, over a dozen national and international law enforcement agencies from four continents have worked directly with the FBI to deal with child sexual exploitation. This program has a high profile within the United States, with three Innocent Images Initiative suspects having been placed on the FBI's Ten Most Wanted Fugitives list since 2000.

TOP 10 TIPS FOR AVOIDING ONLINE PREDATORS

1. Talk with your child about the potential dangers of online child predators.
2. Spend time together when your child is online to become familiar with your child's online habits.
3. Arrange the computers in your home so that the screen is visible to other members of the family.
4. Encourage your child to tell you if he or she is ever made uncomfortable or scared by something experienced online.
5. Make sure you have the user names, passwords, and other information needed to review any of your child's online activities.
6. Occasionally review your child's online activities, including the contents of any online accounts.

7. Occasionally review your child's use of offline communications such as telephones, cell phones, and regular mail.
8. Make sure your child understands your family's rules for being online, and that the rules apply at home and away from home.
9. Closely supervise any risky online activities such as chat rooms, file sharing, and webcams.
10. Immediately report suspected child predators to the appropriate law enforcement organization.

CHAPTER 8

EMAIL BASICS

In This Chapter
- An Overview of Email
- Email Etiquette
- The Gettysburg Criterion
- Top 10 Email Realities

Of all the applications on the Internet, email is the most popular, and perhaps the most important. If your child can master the basics of email, she will probably have a very easy time working with any other kind of online communication. One reason for email's importance is that it is an application that almost everyone who is online will use regularly. Included in this chapter are the following:

- A description of the basic parts of an email.
- A top ten list of tips for more effective email.
- Advice on when it is appropriate to either send or respond to email.
- An overview of email attachments and suggestions for how to use attachments effectively.
- A review of responsible email behavior.

- Examples of how to send email so the recipient clearly understands the message.

An Overview of Email

Email is a generic term for messages composed and transmitted on a computer network. It can be accessed through a personal computer program or through one of the many online email services such as Gmail and Yahoo! Mail. No matter what program or service your child uses for email, they all share these common features:

- A field for the body of the message.
- A field for the subject line.
- A "From" field that indicates the email address of the sender of a message.
- Addressing options that allow up to three different kinds of recipients.
- An option to have a customized signature block for every outgoing email.
- The option of attaching one or more files to be sent along with a text message.

Addressing Options

There are three areas or fields where your child can place a recipient's address: the "To" field, the "Cc" field (carbon copy), or the "Bcc" (blind carbon copy) field. The best option to use depends on the kind of email your child is sending and the number of recipients:

- **Use the "To" field**: Use this option for a single recipient or for multiple recipients if everyone already knows one another's email address.

- **Use the "To" field and the "Cc" field**: Use this combination for multiple recipients. The people in the "To" field should need to either to take some action or use the information in the message. The people in the "Cc" field need to be aware of the information, but do not need to take any action.
- **Use the "Bcc" field**: Use this option if there are multiple recipients, and the recipients do not need to know the addresses of at least some of the other recipients. All the recipients in the "Bcc" field will be able to see the addresses in the "To" or the "Cc" field, and no recipient will be able to see any of the addresses in the "Bcc" field.

SUBJECT LINE

One of the most important parts of an email message is the subject line. Upon opening most email programs, the sender's email address and the subject line are the only parts of the email a recipient sees. Most recipients decide whether to read the email based on what the subject line says. The best kind of subject line is like the headline of a newspaper — it is clear, concise, and encourages the reader to check out the rest of the story. Encourage your child to always use the subject line, and to follow these general rules:

- Clearly describe what the email is about.
- Keep it short, using no more than about ten words (about 50 characters, including spaces).
- Use acronyms, words, or phrases that would be familiar to the recipient.
- Use appropriate language.

BAD IDEAS FOR SUBJECT LINES

A good subject line encourages the recipient to read an email, and a bad one encourages the recipient to delete it. Any email that looks like it is unsolicited, unwanted, or inappropriate will likely not get opened. Make sure your child does not get into any of the following habits:

- Sending email with blank subject lines.
- Using multiple exclamation points!!!, question marks??? or special %&#$@* characters.
- Using obscene or sexually oriented language.
- Using threatening language.
- Using language that is not appropriate for an educational or professional environment.
- USING ALL CAPITAL LETTERS.
- Using words or phrases associated with fraudulent schemes, chain letters, or other common types of unsolicited email.

THE EMAIL BODY

The body of an email is either a plain text message or a formatted HTML document with text, graphics, and links to Internet resources. Your child's email program should be set up to only create and send plain text messages so that the message can be read by any email program.

The typical body of an email is relatively short, from one sentence to about one page of text or other material. Longer messages or ones containing something other than plain text should be sent as an email attachment.

While there are no formal rules on what kind of information should be in the body of an email, the following are common informal rules are followed in plain text emails:

- Double spacing is used to separate paragraphs.
- Paragraphs are not indented.
- The message is written using standard rules of capitalization and grammar.
- Words written in bold type in a regular letter (such as headlines) are written in CAPITAL LETTERS.

ATTACHMENTS

An attachment is a file that is sent as part of an email message. You should teach your child to take the following precautions when sending attachments:

- **Send an attachment only if necessary**: If a plain text message will do, your child should not send an attachment.
- **Send only to those who need it**: If your child is not sure whether the recipient needs the file, have your child ask the recipient if he or she wants it.
- **Send only to those who are expecting it**: Teach your child to avoid sending attachments when the recipient is not expecting one. Your child should first get permission from the recipient.
- **Make sure the recipient can open the attachment**: Only send an attachment if you know the recipient has a program that can open the file.
- **Send the smallest file possible**: Many ISPs have a limit on the size of an email attachment. Most should accept files smaller than one megabyte.

ORGANIZING EMAIL

Emails are files that are typically saved in a format that is specific to the email program or online email service that you are using. You usually have to use that particular program or service to find old emails.

Most email programs and online email services use a file structure similar to what is used in the Windows Explorer file management program. Your child should be able to create folders, give the folders descriptive names, and move emails into appropriate folders. In Windows Explorer, a folder acts as the index for the files it contains, and may include information such as the name of a file, the size of a file, and the file's creation date. Within an email program, folders perform a similar function for groups of emails.

If your child uses more than one email program or online email account, she will either have to do email management in several places, or make sure that all of her emails are in one convenient place. There are several options for consolidating emails:

- When using a secondary email account, use the "Bcc" field to send a copy of each outgoing email to the primary account.
- Set up each secondary account to automatically forward a copy of any incoming email to the primary account. A forwarded email is one that is received by one person and then sent out again to one or more other recipients, and with no significant changes to the original content.
- Set up the primary email account so it can access secondary email accounts and download any new incoming emails.

EMAIL ACCESS ISSUES

Any personal computer that is equipped to access the Internet usually has several options for email, including an email account supplied by your ISP or free online email accounts. If your child has several email accounts, she may be able to have incoming email from one account forwarded to another, or be able to access one account while using another account.

HOW MANY EMAIL ADDRESSES ARE ENOUGH?

Once your child starts using email regularly, it would be a good idea to have one primary email address and three kinds of secondary email addresses:

- **Primary address**: This is an almost private account that your child should use only with family, a few trusted friends, and for school-related business.
- **Administrative address**: This is an address your child should use for online services, to sign up for mailing lists, and for similar activities. If your child is given a special-purpose account—for example, a school email account—it should only be used for that special purpose.
- **Throwaway address**: As the name suggests, this is an email address that your child could simply stop using if she has problems like too much unsolicited email. This is the safest kind of address your child can post online.
- **Backup address**: This is an address that will only be used to as a replacement if there is a problem with an actively used address.

Free Web-Based Email

There are a number of free online email accounts your child can use for either a primary or secondary email address. Refer to the "Online Email Accounts" section of appendix 2 for descriptions of some of these services. These accounts may be convenient, but they usually have a few drawbacks, including little or no customer service and no guarantee that the service will remain free.

Abbreviations, Acronyms, and Slang

Schools, businesses, and organizations routinely use email for written communications, so your child should learn to treat an email the same way that she would treat a regular letter. That means she should follow normal rules for grammar, spelling, and punctuation.

When it comes to writing effective email messages, the same grammar and common-sense rules that apply in other written communication apply to email. Using abbreviations, acronyms, and slang may be an easy way for your child to communicate with friends or classmates, but she should not do this for two reasons. First, the abbreviations, acronyms, and slang that are perfectly understandable today may look confusing or silly next month or next year. The second reason is that email has become an acceptable way to send formal written correspondence, and acronyms and slang are often not appropriate for this kind of communication.

Having a family rule that email should be written in normal English is a good way to get children into writing habits that will benefit them for a lifetime. As a compromise, you may allow a more informal writing style for IM or chat rooms.

EMAIL ETIQUETTE

When it comes to the socially acceptable ways to send email, no one set of rules will work in every situation, but the following suggestions for email etiquette will probably work most of the time:

- Always check formatting, grammar, and spelling.
- Avoid sending jokes or other kinds of humor. If the recipient is insulted, the email provides written proof that can be used against the sender.
- Don't forward other people's messages without permission.
- Don't send attachments unless you need to.
- Keep emails as short as possible, but as long as necessary.
- Never put anything in an email that would be embarrassing if it were printed on the front page of the newspaper.
- Send an email only if there is something worth saying.
- Use the subject line to give a brief description of the contents of the message.
- When forwarding email, do not forward other people's email addresses.
- When responding to a message, include enough of the previous message so the recipient understands the context of the response.
- When sending a message to multiple recipients, consider using the blind carbon copy address field so the recipients do not see all of the other email addresses.

THE GETTYSBURG CRITERION

Emails tend to be short, rather than long. While there is no specific rule about the maximum length of an email, there is one historical example that provides a guide for today.

President Abraham Lincoln's address at the dedication of the cemetery at Gettysburg, PA, on November 19, 1863 was a speech of only 266 words that was both a powerful message on the principles of democratic government and a shining example of how a short message can speak volumes. This speech also provides the inspiration for the Gettysburg Criterion—that the text in the body of an email should be shorter than the Gettysburg Address.

To use the Gettysburg Criterion, email a copy of the Gettysburg Address to your child, and then have your child print the email. Whenever your child is drafting an email that seems a bit long, compare it with the Gettysburg Address email. If the draft is longer than Lincoln's speech, then shorten the text. If making it shorter is not an option, then your child should consider sending the message in an attached file. Here is the text of the Gettysburg Address inscribed in the Lincoln Memorial in Washington, DC (punctuation added for clarity):

> Fourscore and seven years ago our fathers brought forth on this continent a new nation, conceived in liberty and dedicated to the proposition that all men are created equal.
>
> Now we are engaged in a great civil war, testing whether that nation or any nation so conceived and so dedicated can long endure. We are met on a great battlefield of that war. We have come to dedicate a portion of that field as a final resting

place for those who here gave their lives that that nation might live. It is altogether fitting and proper that we should do this.

But in a larger sense, we can not dedicate, we can not consecrate, we can not hallow, this ground. The brave men, living and dead, who struggled here have consecrated it far above our poor power to add or detract. The world will little note nor long remember what we say here, but it can never forget what they did here. It is for us the living, rather, to be dedicated here to the unfinished work which they who fought here have thus far so nobly advanced. It is rather for us to be here dedicated to the great task remaining before us—that from these honored dead we take increased devotion to that cause for which they gave the last full measure of devotion—that we here highly resolve that these dead shall not have died in vain; that this nation, under God, shall have a new birth of freedom; and that government of the people, by the people, for the people shall not perish from the earth.

The Gettysburg Criterion is only one way to evaluate your child's writing. If she writes an email that is long but effective, don't force her to make it shorter or put it into an attachment. But if using the Gettysburg Criterion encourages you and your child to take the time to talk about writing, it will probably help both of you in ways that go far beyond that particular email.

TOP 10 EMAIL REALITIES

1. **Email is an insecure communication**: Treat an email like a postcard and assume that someone other than the recipient will be able to read it.
2. **Email can't be recalled**: Once an email has been sent, it is out of the sender's control.
3. **Email is forever**: The sender, the recipient, and any computer system involved with transmitting the email may have copies, and there is no way of knowing how long those copies will stay around.
4. **Email should be treated seriously**: Many of the laws and traditions associated with written correspondence apply to email.
5. **The contents of an email may be copyrighted**: This means that the person who wrote the email can control how it can be used. This is true for the United States and for countries with similar copyright laws.
6. **Not every email you receive deserves a response**: If a response is not expected or not required, don't respond.
7. **Not every recipient of your email will send a response**: If a response is expected, ask the recipient to send one.
8. **Free speech has its limits**: The regulations and laws that limit free expression apply to email.
9. **Pay attention to the rules**: Be aware of the rules that your ISP, school, or organization may have about sending and receiving email.
10. **Email is not going away**: Email will likely remain an important method of communication. Make sure your child becomes comfortable with using email and also knows how to use it responsibly.

CHAPTER 9

DEALING WITH UNWANTED EMAIL

In This Chapter
- An Overview of Unwanted Email
- Seven Steps to Controlling Email
- Top 10 Ways to Stop Unwanted Email

Years before there was a World Wide Web, the Internet had email. Sending and receiving email are the most popular activities of Internet users. Unfortunately, much of the email that an average user receives is not useful, not desired, and sometimes downright offensive. This is a problem for anyone who uses email, so one of the earliest online skills your child should learn is how to deal with unwanted email. This chapter will help your child by providing him with practical advice on how to do the following:

- How to recognize unwanted email.
- How to reduce the amount of incoming email.
- How to filter unwanted email.

An Overview of Unwanted Email

Unwanted email includes messages that have malicious software attachments, are part of some kind of fraudulent scheme, or are associated with cyberbullying, online child predators, or other illegal or undesirable activities. Chapter 7 discussed child predator and cyberbullying issues, including the ways predators use email. This chapter focuses on other types of undesirable email:

- Email that makes demands on your time and energy, but provides little or no benefit.
- Email that has potentially harmful attachments.
- Email that encourages visits to web sites associated with malicious software, fraudulent activity, or inappropriate content.
- Unsolicited commercial email.

Why Learn About Unwanted Email?

Every minute your child spends with unwanted email is precious time taken away from more productive uses of the Internet. If you take time to show your child how to deal with this problem, you will make his time online more worthwhile.

The Difference Between Spam and Unwanted Email

Spam is the popular term for unsolicited commercial email. The term may also be applied to unsolicited email containing chain letters, bogus offers, rumors, and other information that lacks authority, usefulness, or validity. Unwanted email includes spam, but also includes situations where there has been a previous relationship with the sender.

How Unwanted Email Ends Up in Your Inbox

There are a number of sources of unwanted email, some of which can be controlled:

- Any business, organization, or individual who has ever received an email from your child.
- Any business, organization, or individual who has ever sent an email to your child.
- Any business, organization, or online service that has ever obtained your child's email address.
- Any mailing lists that your child has ever joined.
- Any web site or other online resource that displays your child's email address.

Categories of Unwanted Email

It is up to your child to control what email gets opened. You should be very clear about what he is allowed to receive and what he is allowed to open. There are several kinds of email you should not allow your children to accept:

- **Adult-oriented**: Emails that contain text or pictures intended for adults; that promote activities, products, services, and intended for adults; or that contain links to adult-oriented online resources.
- **Chain letters, jokes, rumors, gossip, and other diversions**: These kinds of emails are not meant to be malicious, but they are usually a distraction.
- **Email with unexpected attachments**: It does not matter whether the email appears to be from a familiar source. You should insist that your child avoids opening these kinds of attachments until someone can confirm the attachment is legitimate.

- **Money making offers**: Usually associated with fraudulent activity, these emails usually promise either quick profits or large profits for little or no effort.
- **Requests for sensitive personal data**: A parent should always respond to this kind of request.

Chain Letters and the Internet

Chain letters were around long before there was an Internet, and follow a predictable formula, typically promising a very positive result if you forward the message to others. Children are prone to the kind of peer pressure that will lead them to forward a chain letter email sent by a friend or classmate. If you discover your child is creating or forwarding chain letters, take the time to explain that sending chain letters is not appropriate.

SEVEN STEPS TO CONTROLLING EMAIL

As long as you have an email address, there will be someone willing to send your child email he does not want to read. However, you can help your child reduce the amount of incoming unwanted email by helping him do the following:

1. Make email less visible online.
2. Make email less visible offline.
3. Filter email before it arrives.
4. Use filters in the email program.
5. Review each email before opening.
6. Learn how to respond to unwanted email.
7. Avoid contributing to unwanted email.

STEP 1: MAKE EMAIL LESS VISIBLE ONLINE

Your child's chances of getting unwanted email go up every time he uses his email. There are several things you can help him do to make his inbox a less attractive target:

- **Choose mailing lists carefully**: Encourage your child to join only mailing lists that send out useful and worthwhile information Also, your child should only join mailing lists that have an easy procedure for removing an address.
- **Avoid having an email address published online**: If your child has to put an address on a web page, use a secondary address. He should still make it hard for automated email-gathering programs to read the address. One trick is to add a space after and before the "@"sign in the address. A human would have the good sense to remove the blanks, but a program would not.
- **Do not sign up for an online service that sends unsolicited email**: When considering a free online service, review the user agreement carefully with your child and only allow him to sign up if the online service allows users the option of declining unsolicited email.
- **Use a secondary email address for administrative purposes**: When registering software or signing up for a new service, sometimes an administrative email address is needed. Encourage your child to use a secondary email address for these purposes, since over time a business that promises not to send any unsolicited email may change its policies.
- **Use a secondary email address for marketing offers**: Online marketers frequently use contests,

coupon offers, and other enticements to get users to provide their email addresses and other contact information. It is very likely that an email address will end up in one or more mailing lists, so remind your child to use a secondary address.
- **Remove your email address from mailing lists**: Remind your child to remove his email address from any mailing list that sends mailings he no longer wants or needs.

STEP 2: MAKE YOUR EMAIL LESS VISIBLE OFFLINE

Schools, government organizations, and businesses may routinely request your child's email address. Teach your child to keep the following in mind when someone asks for his email address:

- If an email is needed for administrative or contact purposes, use a secondary email address.
- If it is not required, do not provide it.
- If someone insists on being provided with an email address, but there is no legal obligation to do so, encourage your child to provide a fake address or an old one he no longer checks.

STEP 3: FILTER YOUR EMAIL BEFORE IT ARRIVES

There are two easy ways to filter your child's email before it reaches her inbox. One way is to have her use at least one secondary email address for all the messages that are not that important. Another way is to have her set up her primary email account to block or filter at least some of her unwanted email.

USING SECONDARY EMAIL ADDRESSES

There are many companies offering free online email accounts that could be used for one or more secondary email addresses. It is a good idea to have a backup just in case your primary account is unavailable, but it is also useful to have one for every day use. Using a free email account for your secondary email address can have several advantages; one of the biggest is that if unwanted mail is a problem, your child can simply stop using the account and get another one. The ideal secondary account has the following characteristics:

- It's free.
- It can be accessed using the Web.
- It allows you to download messages into your home computer's email program.
- It has spam filters as well as the ability to filter email by address or by content.

One drawback of many free email services is that the account may be deleted after a period of inactivity. If your child is going to access the account at least once a month, this should not be a problem.

SET UP FILTERS ON THE PRIMARY EMAIL ADDRESS

Typically, anyone who uses an ISP to access the Internet from home is given one or more email addresses. Most ISPs have a basic level of filtering to eliminate spam and other emails that are considered malicious, fraudulent, or objectionable. Check with your ISP to see what kinds of filtering are possible for the account your child uses.

Step 4: Use Filters in Your Email Program

Typically, a program like Outlook Express is used to send and receive mail through your primary email account. Outlook Express and similar programs have the ability to filter emails by either deleting them before your child downloads them from the server, or by deleting after they arrive. These kinds of filters are most convenient for doing the following kinds of actions:

- Blocking emails with objectionable words.
- Blocking emails from specific addresses.
- Blocking emails with very large attachments.
- Directing email from particular addresses into a folder other than the inbox.

Setting Up Filters in Outlook Express

Outlook Express has numerous options for filtering unwanted emails or directing email into folders. You or your child can set up the filter by doing the following:

1. Select **Tools** from the menu bar.
2. Select **Message Rules** from the pull-down menu.
3. Select **Mail…** from the available options, which will open the **Message Rules** dialog box.
4. Select either the **Mail Rules** tab to create rules for incoming mail or the **Blocked Senders** tab to block incoming email from particular addresses.

Be sure to refer to your documentation or to the help files for specific instructions on how to create filters or block senders. If your child uses another program or an online account to manage email, she can review the appropriate help files for directions on how to proceed.

USING ADDITIONAL FILTERING SOFTWARE

You can also add software to your home computer that can filter incoming email. Unlike the filtering options within Outlook Express or within a free Web-based email service, it will cost money to acquire and maintain the software. Before spending money on additional software or services, you and your child should use the free tools that are already available to you.

STEP 5: SCAN INCOMING EMAIL

No matter how careful your child may be when it comes to avoiding and filtering unwanted email, some will always get through. Your child has to be able to spot suspicious email and delete it because such mail may contain content that may be disturbing to your child and perhaps hazardous to your computer.

SETTING UP HOW YOUR INBOX IS DISPLAYED

It is usually easy to spot an unwanted email by simply checking out the sender, the subject line, and perhaps the first few lines of text. The email program that your child uses should be set up to display some or all of this information. To set up Outlook Express, do the following:

1. Choose **View** from the menu bar.
2. Choose **Layout...** from the pull-down menu, which will open the **Window Layout Properties** dialog box.
3. To see only the sender and the subject line, make sure the **Show Preview Pane** check box is unchecked.

4. To see the first few lines of any email that you select, make sure the **Show Preview Pane** check box is checked.
5. If any changes were made, select **Apply** to check the main Outlook Express display.
6. When done, select **OK** to close the dialog box.

If you use an email program other than Outlook Express, review the documentation and help files to see how you can set up your display.

Spotting an Unwanted Email

If your child is allowed to check email without adult supervision, make sure that she knows that emails with one or more of the following warning signs should be deleted without first being opened:

- The email, whether sent by a stranger or from a familiar address, has an unexpected attachment.
- The email is from a stranger and the subject line contains random words or characters.
- The sender is unfamiliar and the subject line is blank.
- The subject line indicates that the email probably has inappropriate content.
- The subject line is in an unfamiliar language.
- The subject line says that you have won some kind of contest or lottery.
- The subject line uses threatening language.
- The subject line warns that you are in some kind of trouble or danger.

Step 6: How to Respond to Unwanted Email

How your child should respond to an unwanted email will depend on the relationship your child has with the sender and on the nature of the email:

- **The email involves illegal activities such as child pornography or is associated with cyberbullying or other kinds of harassment**: You and your child should follow the advice given in chapter 7 on cyberbullies and child predators.
- **The email is from a person who has some kind of continuing offline relationship with your child**: You or your child should ask that person to stop sending that kind of email.
- **The email is from an organization, group, or online service that has a relationship with your child**: If your child does not want to receive any more emails, she could request that no further emails be sent. If emails still arrive, take action to block any emails from that source.
- **The sender is unknown and the email is only a slight inconvenience**: Most unwanted email falls into this category. Your child should ignore this type of email. Any response will likely generate additional unwanted email.
- **The email was sent from your child's school**: Contact the school to deal with this issue. Find out what actions the school plans to take and follow up to make sure the actions are taken.

What to Do if the Problem Gets Serious

When the amount of unwanted email becomes so great that it takes up too much of your child's computer time, or if the type of mail that is coming in is so disturbing or objectionable that you do not want to even look at them, then you should change email addresses. If the problem was with a free online email account, simply use another one. if the problem account is associated with your ISP, contact that ISP to get a new email address. Most ISPs allow you to have multiple email addresses on the same account, so there is no need to stop using an ISP just because of a problem with one of those addresses.

STEP 7: DO NOT CONTRIBUTE TO THE PROBLEM
Parents should provide guidance for their children regarding how to properly and responsibly use email. Part of that effort includes encouraging your child to create effective emails. You and your child should work together to learn how to follow at least some of the following good habits:

1. **Keep messages short**: Shorter messages are more likely to be completely read than long messages.
2. **Have a good reason for sending an email**: If the recipient does not have an immediate use for the information in the email, don't send it.
3. **Use a clear and descriptive subject line**: Badly written subject lines look too much like spam.
4. **Use appropriate spelling and grammar**: If your email program has a spell checker, use it. Also, an email written with proper spelling and grammar is more likely to be read and understood.
5. **Send email only to people who need to see it**: An email with a long list of recipients in the "To" or "Cc" fields may not be seen as urgent as one addressed to an individual or small group.

6. **Use the blind carbon copy field when sending email to groups of people**: If the recipients have no need to know each other's email addresses, protect everyone's privacy by using the "Bcc" field.
7. **Think twice before forwarding**: Forward an email only if the recipient really needs to see it. Any forwarded email should include a short note at the beginning that explains why the message was sent.

TOP 10 WAYS TO STOP UNWANTED EMAIL

1. **Don't volunteer to receive email**: Unless there is a good reason to receive email, just say no.
2. **Have one or more secondary addresses for less important emails**: If unwanted email becomes a problem, move to another secondary address.
3. **Use your primary email address only for people and organizations that you trust**: If a sender's habits change for the worse, provide that sender with a secondary address.
4. **Don't put your primary email address online**: Use a secondary address instead.
5. **Use the blind carbon copy field for multiple recipients**: Since each recipient can only see addresses that are in the "To" or "Cc" fields, put your address in the "To" field and all the recipients in the "Bcc" field.
6. **Encourage any group that sends you email to use blind carbon copy**: Contact the person responsible for sending the group's emails and explain how to use the "Bcc" field.

7. **Send unsolicited email only when necessary**: Don't send an email unless the recipient has a good reason to read or respond to the message.
8. **Don't respond to unsolicited commercial email**: Responding to the email or to the commercial offer in any way will likely encourage more unsolicited emails.
9. **Treat the subject line like a newspaper headline**: Summarize the email in less than ten words. An email with a well-written subject line is less likely to be accidentally ignored and deleted.
10. **Teach your child how to recognize and respond to unwanted emails**: Your child should learn to delete unwanted email and to get you involved if the email involves issues that should be addressed by an adult.

CHAPTER 10

WEB BASICS

In This Chapter
- A Quick Overview of a Web Site
- Basic Kinds of Web Sites
- How to Use Search Engines and Directories
- Top 10 Search Engine and Directory Tips
- Finding the Key Sites on a Particular Subject
- Top 10 Tips for Using the Web

Your child has to understand how to use the World Wide Web if she wants to get the most out of being online. The Web is huge, with hundreds of millions of web sites and billions of web pages. Whether she is online for school or for fun, she has to know how to find the pages and the sites that will give her the information she needs, and she has to know how to do that without wasting a lot of time. This chapter will show her how to do those things by explaining all the steps she needs to find the most important web sites on a particular subject.

A QUICK OVERVIEW OF A WEB SITE

A web site is nothing more than a collection of files residing on a computer that is connected to the World Wide Web. Web sites usually contain information in the form of text and graphics, but may also have information in other media like video files. The more recent versions of Firefox and Internet Explorer can access all of the data on most web sites, especially those sites that only contain text and simple graphics.

What makes a web site particularly useful is its ability to take a user from one page to another online resource. These links, also known as hypertext links or hyperlinks, can take a user to another part of the page, another part of the site, or to a completely different web site with one click of the mouse. These links allow a well-designed web site to be a very flexible tool that can connect you to the best available online resources.

Basic Kinds of Web Sites

While a page within a web site is usually focused on one subject, the entire site may have a broader purpose. Most sites fit into one or more of the following categories:

- **Informational**: These sites provide information on a particular subject. The information is often a combination of data within the site and links to related information outside of the site.
- **Organizational support**: These sites are designed to support an organization. Sites run by schools or businesses often fall into this category.
- **Personal**: These sites are focused on the activities or accomplishments of an individual.
- **Promotional**: This kind of site presents mostly positive information about a person, product, concept, or service. Commercial sites selling goods or services fall into this category. Also falling into

this category are sites that advocate some kind of political, organizational, or social position.
- **Service**: These sites support some online service such as email or search engines.

STRUCTURE AND ORGANIZATION OF A WEB SITE

Most sites are organized around a home page that has one or more of the following:

- Links to related resources outside of the site.
- Links to key pages within the site.
- A link to an internal search engine.
- A link to an index or table of contents page.

For example, AirSafe.com is a web site about airline safety. Individual web pages are devoted to specific airlines or aircraft types. The home page acts as a table of contents, with most of the links going directly to a page that deals with one area of the site. There is also an internal search engine link on most pages, including the home page.

PROBLEMS WITH USING INFORMATION ON THE WEB

Just because something is on a web site does not mean it is either true or useful. Before your child uses a web site for something like a school project, she should understand that she has to figure out whether the web site can be trusted. Your child should learn how to keep the following issues in mind when using web sites:

- **Authority**: You child should verify that people who have the appropriate kinds of experience, credentials, or knowledge run the site.

- **Detail**: Most web sites only show a small part of the information available on a subject.
- **Legal standing**: A web site, even a site managed by a responsible or respected individual or group, should not be considered the official or legally binding version of that information.
- **Longevity**: A web site can be changed, moved, or eliminated at any time and without warning.
- **Standards**: There are no widely accepted or widely enforced standards for the content, format, quality, or organization of web sites.
- **Technical limitations**: Your computer may not be able to properly display all of the contents of a web site.

Of all these problems, the lack of standards for the quality of content on the Web is the most critical one for students. If you want your child to be able to easily find sites and to evaluate if the sites are worth using, then your child should become familiar with the information in the rest of this chapter.

How to Use Search Engines and Directories

Unlike a library, the Web is not organized in any logical way. The number of web sites and web pages is so large that anyone who uses the Web needs to have a tool in order to quickly find information. Fortunately, search engines and directories are two online tools that make it easy to find information. This section of the book provides a general overview of how search engines and directories work, and provides specific advice on using different kinds of search engines for different tasks. A few of the more important definitions include the following:

- **Directory**: An online service that organizes links to Internet resources by category or by some other criteria.
- **Keyword**: A word used within a search engine to locate resources online.
- **Key phrase**: A group of words, typically enclosed by quotation marks, that are used within a search engine the way that keywords are used.
- **Search engine**: An online service that allows a user to find Web-based resources by using one or more keywords or key phrases to describe the desired information.

Unlike a good librarian, a search engine can't use judgment or ask questions to figure out what you need. How well a search engine or a directory works depends on what you tell it to do. In general, the difference between a search engine and directory is that a search engine automatically scans and evaluates a web site. For a directory, human beings evaluate the web sites. Another difference is that a directory arranges information by category. For both a directory and a search engine, a user must start with a goal in mind.

Most search engines have a home page that features an input field for search engine commands that is called a search box. A user types in one or more keywords or key phrases for a basic search and perhaps some logic commands for a more complex search. Most directories have a home page that acts like a table of contents, with links on that home page for each major category. Like a search engine home page, the typical directory home page has a search box allowing a user to search the directory using keywords and key phrases.

How to Search Using Google

The following description provides an explanation of how to use the Google search engine. Google is the most popular search engine on the Web, and the internal search engines of many web sites use its technology. If your child can understand the basics of this search engine, he or she will easily learn how to use other search engines.

Capitalization Does Not Matter

Google's search engine ignores capitalization. Also, if a search request has more than one word, the search engine looks for results containing all of the words. For example, the search command [Shakespeare Hamlet] tells that search engine look only for those entries containing both words (the brackets signify the entries in the search box). The results would be the same if the search terms were [Shakespeare hamlet], [shakespeare Hamlet], or even [shakespeare hamlet].

Order Does Matter

The order of the words will change the result. The search request [space shuttle] gives different results than the search request [shuttle space]. Search terms should be in the order that makes the most sense. To find results containing a specific phrase, enclose that phrase in quotation marks. For example [space shuttle problem] will get more results than, ["space shuttle problem"] because the results of the first search will include online resources that contain the three words anywhere in the document, and the results of the second search will include only those resources that contain the phrase "space shuttle problem."

Word Variations Are Included Automatically

Google and most other search engines will look for the search terms as well as for words that are similar to the search terms. A search for [africa airline] may turn up resources containing the words "African" and "airlines."

Common Words Are Ignored

The Google search engine ignores commonly used words and single digit numbers. There are two ways to keep this from happening: include the common word or the single digit number as part of a key phrase, or place a plus sign in front of the common word or single digit number.

How to Exclude Words or Phrases

To exclude a word or a phrase from the search results, put a minus sign in front of the word or phrase. For example, a search for [airline safety -Airbus] will give results that include the words "airline" or "safety" but that do not include the name "Airbus."

Advanced Search Features

Most search engines have advanced features that allow more specific searches. There is usually a link near the search box or submit button that leads to a detailed explanation of the rules for basic searches and the options for advanced searches. Some of the more useful advanced search options for the Google search engine include the following:

- **Either one term or the other**: Inserting the word "OR" in uppercase between two search terms will give results that contain either term or both terms.

For example, [airline OR safety] provides resources containing either one or both words.
- **Searches within a web site**: Using the operator "site:" in front of a domain name limits search results to that particular web site. For example, [site:airsafe.com midair collision] will return those resources within the site AirSafe.com that contain the words "midair" and "collision."
- **Sites that link to a web page**: Placing the operator "link:" in front of the URL of a web page will generate a list of resources that link to that page.

STARTING AND REFINING A SEARCH

There are two parts to any search: understanding what is needed and then going out and finding it. This often involves doing several searches, refining the search each time to get better results. Depending on the results, your child may have to broaden the search, narrow the search, or take the search in a new direction.

Before the Search

Your child should take the time to figure out what he wants to find, and think of a few words or phrases that best describe what he wants to find. After that, he can take the following steps:

- Start by using general keywords or key phrases in the initial searches on a particular subject. For example, [airplane airline united] is a more general search than [747 United]. Based on the results of the initial searches, either broaden or narrow subsequent searches.

- To broaden a search, remove at least one keyword from the request, use a minus sign to exclude a word or phrase, or remove the quotation marks from a key phrase. For example, changing a search form [airplane United] to [airplane] or from ["United Airlines"] to [United Airlines] will return additional entries.
- To narrow a search, include additional keywords or key phrases, or use a more precise keyword or key phrase. For example, the search [United 747] will return fewer results than [United].
- To take the search in a new direction, replace search terms with words or phrases from related concepts or by using synonyms for the search terms. To find synonyms, use a printed thesaurus or an online thesaurus such as the ones described in appendix 2. For example, the search [United airliner] will give results similar to the search [United aircraft].

CHOOSING A SEARCH ENGINE OR DIRECTORY

There are many search engine and directory choices on the Web. Picking a search engine or a directory comes down to finding one that best satisfies the user's search needs. The best advice is to try several of the search engines or directories to see which ones are consistently useful. Details of several options are provided in the "Search Engines and Directories" section of appendix 2.

HOW SEARCH ENGINES DISPLAY RESULTS

The result of most queries to a search engine or directory is a listing of resources that usually includes the name of the resource, its URL, and a short description of the resource's contents. Each search engine and directory uses different criteria to rank the results, and will return different results for the same set of keywords or key phrases.

SEARCH ENGINE AND DIRECTORY LIMITATIONS

The key limitation of all search engines and directories is that no single search engine or directory can search the entire contents of the Web. Some web site operators also design their sites so search engines are unable to index some or all of the site.

There are other limitations. For example, when new material is added to a web site, or older material deleted from a site, the database of a search engine or directory may not be immediately updated to reflect that change. As a result, the output of a search engine or directory query may include descriptions of web pages or web sites that may be no longer current, that may be no longer available online, or that may have been moved.

CHILD-FRIENDLY SEARCH ENGINES AND DIRECTORIES

If you want your child to become familiar with using a search engine or directory, but do not want him to encounter inappropriate or objectionable content, you have a couple of choices. One option is to use any filtering options provided by a search engine or directory. Another option is to have him use a search engine or directory that is designed for younger children. Several of those are also listed in the "Search Engines and Directories" section of appendix 2.

Top 10 Search Engine and Directory Tips

1. Have your child try out several search engines and directories to find the ones that produce the best results.
2. Make sure your child reviews the help files or online instructions for a search engine or directory to get an idea of how each one works.
3. Make sure your child can use the advanced features of the search engine or directory.
4. Most search engines ignore capitalization.
5. Remember that no search engine or directory can search for all of the information that is online.
6. Become familiar with the techniques for making a search broader.
7. Become familiar with the techniques for making a search narrower.
8. It may take several searches, each one either narrower or broader than the last, in order to find the desired content.
9. Use two or more search engines or directories to get more complete coverage of a subject.
10. Always have a goal in mind when starting a search.

Finding the Key Sites on a Particular Subject

All web sites are not created equal. Although every site has the potential to enlighten, to entertain, or to inspire, the reality is that only a small percentage of the sites that deal with a particular subject are worthy of even a cursory look. Finding the most valuable sites on a particular topic is worth the time and effort; these are the sites that are most likely to satisfy your child's information needs on a particular subject. Finding these web sites takes a combination of prior knowledge of the subject, insights that others may have about the subject, and the ability to properly use a search engine or directory.

WHAT IS A KEY WEB SITE

A key web site is one that provides a level of information or a level of service that is better than most or all of the available alternatives. The previous section of this chapter discussed how to use a search engine or directory to find useful information on a subject. This section goes further, describing how to find a site that provides information or services that are superior to most or all of the available alternatives. This kind of site should have many of the following characteristics:

- Links from the site go to resources that provide complementary information or services.
- News organizations frequently refer to the site.
- Related key sites also link back to the site.
- The information on the site is kept current.
- The information or service provided on the site is superior to competing sites.
- The site can serve as a reliable reference resource.
- The site does not contain significant factual or grammatical errors.

HOW TO FIND KEY SITES

Finding out what sites may be key for a particular subject can be broken down into a four-step process:

1. Take the time to write down what is known about the services or information being sought.

2. Find potential key sites using search engines and directories.
3. Evaluate each potential site to determine which ones deserve further consideration.
4. Carefully review the remaining sites for the quality of their content and the quality of the sites that are linked back to them.

WRITE DOWN WHAT IS WANTED

If you want your child to learn how to consistently find the best web sites about any particular subject, get her into the habit of first writing down what she knows about a subject before going online. If she knows nothing about that subject, she should get some idea about it from a reference book or from a knowledgeable person. The "Encyclopedias and General References" section of appendix 2 lists several online resources she could use. She should identify the most prominent groups, organizations, and individuals that have an ongoing involvement in the subject. She should also be able to describe what she is looking for as precisely as possible.

START SEARCHING

The next step is for your child to develop a list of keywords and key phrases that are based on her initial research and to use them to conduct an online search. If initial searches are not satisfactory, she can either broaden or narrow the search using the techniques described earlier in the chapter. She may also want to try a different search engine or directory.

An important part of any search strategy is knowing which leads to follow and which ones to ignore. The following general rules should be helpful to your child:

- If a resource appears to be from a personal site, your child should ignore it unless she was looking for that person's ideas or opinions.
- If the sponsor of the site is an organization with a significant offline presence, that site is a better candidate for further investigation.
- If the description of the resource contains most or all of the search keywords or key phrases, that site is worth a closer look.
- Your child should focus on recently updated sites unless the information she child wants is either historical data or information that does not change frequently.
- If your child does not find any useful results in the first three to five pages of search results, she should try a different set of search terms, a different search engine, or a different directory.

Once you have a list of candidate sites, the next step is to find out which of these sites contain key information. This kind of site will have one or more of the following characteristics:

- Other key sites will have links back to the site.
- The site has links to other key sites.
- The site provides a superior level of information or a superior level of service.

There are several techniques your child should use to determine whether a site has these characteristics. The following section provides the details on how that should be done.

JUDGING THE QUALITY OF A WEB SITE

If a site provides a service, you child can judge the quality by using the service. For a site that primarily provides information, your child will have to check to see if it contains the specific information needed to address her particular needs. The steps in this process are as follows:

- Establish the legitimacy of the site.
- Judge the value of the information or the service.
- Evaluate the site's ease of use.
- Evaluate the links from a site.
- Evaluate the links to a site.

Establishing the Legitimacy of the Site

The first step of establishing its legitimacy is to determine whether the individual or group responsible for the site has the authority or the capacity to discuss the subject matter covered by the site or to provide the services offered by the site. For sites managed by an individual or organization that is widely recognized as an authority on a given subject or the provider of a given service, this step may not be unnecessary. For other sites, your child has to determine if the provider of the information or service is credible. Sites meeting most or all of the following criteria are likely to be a credible source of information:

- The organization or individual that operates the site is easily identifiable.
- The site is authorized to provide the information or service.
- The organization or individual responsible for the information or services provided by the site is qualified by experience, expertise, or credentials.

- The reputation of the person or group responsible for the site would be damaged if the information on the site were not accurate or credible, or if the level of service provided by the site was poor.
- The individual or group that controls the site also has a significant and related offline presence.

Judging the Value of the Information or Service
A high-value informational site should meet most of the following criteria:

- Any audio, animation, graphics, or other complex elements enhance the information on the site.
- Graphs, charts, and other visual displays of data are clearly labeled and easy to interpret.
- Limitations of the data or of the other information on the site are clearly stated.
- The facts on the site can be verified from at least one independent and reputable source.
- The information on the site is consistent with the purpose of the site.
- The information on the site is current.
- The information on the site is as good as or better than similar information from other sources.
- The site clearly describes the method or methods used in any analysis discussed within the site.
- The site contains few, if any, factual errors.
- The site has a clear purpose.
- The site identifies the source or sources of any outside information used on the site.
- The site provides definitions of any acronyms or special terminology used on the site.

- The written content consistently follows basic rules of grammar, spelling, and composition.
- There are no apparent conflicts of interest between the sponsor of the site, the advertisers on the site, and the information on the site.

The value of a service is best judged by using the service. If the service is of high quality, it should also have most of the following characteristics:

- The service can be tailored to meet a user's needs.
- The service is available around the clock.
- The site is not involved in any fraudulent or illegal activity in order to provide the service.
- Users are required to provide little or no personal information in order to use the service.

Evaluating a Site's Ease of Use

An easy-to-use web site should have at least several of the following characteristics:

- Every page of the site links to at least one of the following: the home page, the table of contents, the index page, or an internal search engine.
- Most of the useful information on the site is within two links from the home page.
- The design of the site does not detract from the information or service it provides.
- The information or service can be accessed from the home page.
- The site accepts user feedback.
- The site has a table of contents.
- The site has an in internal search engine.

- The site has an index.
- The site explains how to use the information or service.
- There are links between related information in different parts of the site.

Evaluating the Links from a Site
This part of the evaluation can be combined with the evaluation of a site's contents or service. The goal is to see if the site provides links to resources that enhance the information or services it provides. Useful links could be to pages within the same site or to outside sites. A useful link should have most of the following characteristics:

- The destination of the link is a specific relevant piece of information or a relevant service.
- The link is conveniently placed within the page.
- The outside site has links to other related key sites.
- The text or graphics that make up the link indicate what is at the other end of the link.

Evaluating the Links to a Site
On a web page, it is easy to spot the outbound links. However, it takes the help of a search engine to see what outside links point to a particular site. For example, in Google, the command [link:<URL name>] will show what pages point to that URL. If a site is a key site, inbound links have the following characteristics:

- The links are from sites that are also key sites.
- The links come from recently updated pages.
- They are from sites with relevant information or services.

TOP 10 TIPS FOR USING THE WEB

1. **Have a purpose for every visit to the Web**: Your child should have a clear set of goals each time he or she is online.
2. **Set time limits on each session**: Make sure your child takes an occasional break during an online session.
3. **Find a working environment that works for you**: Make sure your child can work comfortably and with few distractions.
4. **Choose the right equipment and software**: Take the time to find the hardware and software that meets your child's needs.
5. **Avoid bad web sites**: If a site doesn't meet the legitimacy, quality, and the ease-of-use criteria described earlier, look for a site that does.
6. **Use your browser more effectively**: Help your browser load pages faster by blocking popups, advertising, or other things that slow it down.
7. **Use search engines and directories**: Make sure that your child knows how to do a proper search with a search engine or directory.
8. **Use links in a site to find related information**: Get your child into the habit of checking a site's incoming and outgoing links.
9. **Find useful sites from offline sources**: Be on the lookout for interesting sites that may be mentioned in other media such as newspapers or television.
10. **Avoid high-demand times**: The busiest times are weekdays from late morning to early afternoon.

"The Clock is Running" Search Engine Game

One way for your child to build basic skills with a search engine is to turn it into a game. "The Clock is Running" is a treasure hunt game where the treasure is a piece of information. Factual data like historical events, current news events, or quotations work well with this game. The rules are simple—the judge gives the player a target question and then says "the clock is running." The player has to use a search engine to find a web page that has the answer. The winner could be the player who finds the answer first, the one who finds the most authoritative source for the answer, or to the player who best combines a quick answer with an authoritative source. This game works best if you change the rules to fit your child's personality. You can make it a competitive game, a cooperative game, a one-player game, a multi-player game, or any other kind of game that you choose. The objective isn't to win or lose, but to get your child to build search engine skills.

Chapter 11

Avoiding Inappropriate Content

In This Chapter
- What Is Inappropriate Content?
- Exposure to Inappropriate Content
- Filtering Inappropriate Content
- Seven Steps to Control Inappropriate Content
- Top 10 Tips About Inappropriate Content

It is no secret that not everything online is appropriate for children. While the nature of the Internet makes it difficult to keep all inappropriate material from your children, there is a lot you and your family can do to keep exposure to this kind of material to a minimum.

What Is Inappropriate Content?

What is inappropriate is a personal and family decision. Most parents would consider sexually explicit material, material promoting hatred, and material glorifying violence to be inappropriate for their children. The following are only a few examples of this kind of content:

- Adult-oriented stories, discussions, or broadcasts.
- Visual depictions of cruelty to animals.

- Visual depictions of sexual activity.
- Web sites containing graphic violence.
- Web sites promoting the use of illegal drugs.
- Web sites or discussion groups promoting racial, ethnic, or religious intolerance.

Exposure to Inappropriate Content

There are three ways to become exposed to inappropriate content:

1. It is found by accident.
2. It is sought out.
3. It is sent to you.

Other parts of this book, specifically chapter 7 on cyberbullying and child predators, and chapter 9 on unwanted email, provide advice on how to address the first kind of exposure to inappropriate material. This chapter will also discuss accidental exposure, but will focus on the other two ways inappropriate material may end up in your home or in front of your child.

Accidental Exposure to Unwanted Content

Exposure to unwanted web content can happen in three ways:

1. **Using the wrong URL**: A URL is a very specific address for a resource on the Web. A single incorrect character may lead you to a completely different web site.
2. **Deceptive web sites**: These are web sites that are designed to lure unsuspecting visitors.

3. **Careless search techniques**: Sometimes a search engine's output will include many resources that have nothing to do with the intended topic. You have to make the effort review the search results before following a link.

DELIBERATELY SEEKING INAPPROPRIATE CONTENT

Every family has rules about what is allowed and what is not allowed. While accidental exposure to inappropriate material will eventually happen to anyone who is online, such exposures will likely be very rare. However, if your child is regularly visiting places that are off limits, you will likely notice one or more of the following behaviors:

- Being evasive when asked about online activity.
- Going online when no one else is around.
- Hiding flash drives, CD-ROMs or other portable storage devices.
- Quickly closing a window, hiding the screen, or turning off the computer.
- Unusual or inappropriate activity while at the computer.

The following situations may also signal that someone in the family is accessing inappropriate material:

- The browser has bookmarks to inappropriate web sites.
- The browser's history file indicates numerous visits to sites with inappropriate content.
- You find inappropriate material on the computer's hard drive or on portable storage devices.

Filtering Inappropriate Content

One way you can limit exposure to inappropriate or objectionable content is through filtering. Filters consist of software or software settings that limit the content that can be displayed or accessed by a computer. Filters can be used to restrict access to one or more of the following:

- Certain categories of web sites.
- Specific types of online activities.
- Web pages with certain kinds of visual content.
- Web pages containing specific words, phrases, or combinations of words and phrases.
- Web sites within a database of banned sites.

Where Filters Are Used

You can find filters in a variety of places, including:

- **In a computer network**: These are more elaborate installations that may be used by a corporation, school, or library.
- **In a personal computer**: These are made primarily for use in the home.
- **Within a program**: Examples include browsers that may be configured to restrict certain types of activity or certain kinds of content.
- **Within an online service**: Services such as search engines may allow users to set content restrictions.

Filter Limitations

The following are the most common limitations of filters:

Chapter 11—Avoiding Inappropriate Content

- **Lack of updating**: If the database used by the filter to determine what sites to restrict or block has not been updated, new sites will not be blocked.
- **Technological Limitations**: The filter may not be able to block some types of content, or your child finds ways to work around the filter.
- **Overblocking**: A condition where a filter blocks access to sites containing acceptable content.
- **Underblocking**: The filter does not block content that you want it to block.

SEVEN STEPS TO CONTROL INAPPROPRIATE CONTENT

There is no single best way to deal with inappropriate material. The following seven actions will help keep this kind of material away from your family and will help you find out if anyone in your family has been looking at banned material:

1. Enforce family rules on Internet use at home or away from home.
2. Check online accounts.
3. Check portable data storage devices.
4. Use filtering on your online services.
5. Use filtering software on your computer.
6. Check your computer for patterns of unusual or inappropriate activity.
7. Check your computer's hard drive

STEP 1: ENFORCING FAMILY INTERNET USE POLICIES

As mentioned in chapter 2, the two key roles are for the child to play by the parents' rules and for parents to make and enforce those rules. Every situation involving a child being exposed to inappropriate material will be different, but there are two ways you can respond:

1. **Accidental Exposure**: Encourage your child to talk to you whenever she comes across something she should not be seeing online. It will give you a chance to figure out why it happened, to take steps to prevent it from happening again, and to take the time to deal with any questions or issues she may have as a result of the exposure.
2. **Deliberate Exposure**: In this situation, the actions you take should be swift, certain, and severe. At the very least, your child's online access should be severely restricted until she understands that such behavior is not acceptable.

Enforcing family rules on inappropriate content will be easier if the following general rules are included in the Internet use agreement of an older child:

- I understand which sites I can visit and which ones are off limits.
- I will follow these same rules when I am at home, in school, at the library, or at a friend's home.
- If I come across something that is off limits or potentially dangerous, I will tell my parents or another responsible adult.

STEP 2: CHECK ONLINE ACCOUNTS

Chapter 4 on privacy provides several suggestions for maintaining a family's online privacy. One suggestion was to keep track of every family member's online accounts. Doing so will allow you to easily check to see if your child has accessed inappropriate material. Also, if you find out that your child has an account that is not on the list, access the account and check it for inappropriate material. Keep track of all accounts using the "List of Online Activities" form in the Family Forms Pack located at http://forms.speedbrake.com.

STEP 3: CHECK PORTABLE DATA STORAGE DEVICES
One of the suggestions from chapter 5 is that the family maintains a record of where everyone keeps their data. If you come across a device that has not been accounted for, check it for anything out of the ordinary and then add it to the "List of Data Storage Devices" form. It is also part of the Family Forms Pack and is available at the above URL.

STEP 4: USE FILTERING ON YOUR ONLINE SERVICES
You may be able to restrict some kinds of content on some of the online services you and your family use. For example, many of the search engines listed in appendix 2 have filters that will keep some kinds of material from being displayed. Other search engines are either designed for children or do not allow adult-oriented material.

If inappropriate content is a concern, you should only allow your family to use those online resources that allow you to limit objectionable material. One way to keep track of what services your family can access is to use the "List of Online Activities" mentioned in Step 2.

STEP 5: USE FILTERING SOFTWARE ON YOUR COMPUTER
If you use filtering software at home, make sure it is designed to deal with the kinds of content that concern you. You still need to monitor your child's computer use since no filter can block all objectionable content.

Step 6: Check Your Computer

Sometimes, your computer may have evidence of inappropriate activity. Two easy ways to find out are to check your browser's history files and the cookies on your hard drive.

Checking Your Browser's History Files

The history file shows what sites and what pages the browser has visited. For both Internet Explorer and Firefox, selecting the history icon on the toolbar will open up a small window that will display the name of each web site visited. In the newly opened window, if you select a web site name, you can see all the pages that were visited on that site. If you see a suspicious site, check to see whether many pages were visited. If you see several pages under that web site, it is likely that it was not an accidental visit.

One warning sign is seeing no data in the history window during periods when you know that someone was spending a lot of time online. This may indicate that someone may have been trying to hide his or her online activities. Also, if you check the history window before you shut the computer down at night, but notice many new sites when you turn it on in the morning, someone has probably been online after hours.

Setting the Number of Days of Browser History

You can set your browser to track a certain number of days of history. Set this value to at least as long as the time between history reviews. For example, if you check once a week, set it to eight days.

Firefox Settings

To set the number of days for the history file, do this:

1. From the menu bar, choose **Tools**.
2. Choose **Options...** from the pull-down menu to open the **Options** dialog box.
3. Select the **Privacy** tab.
4. In the **History** section, enter the number of days you want the browser to track visited web pages.
5. Select **OK** to close the **Options** dialog box.

Internet Explorer 6 Settings

To set the number of days for the history file, do this:

1. From the menu bar, choose **Tools**.
2. Select **Internet Options...** from the pull-down menu to open the **Internet Options** dialog box.
3. Select the **General** tab.
4. In the **History** section, enter the number of days you want the browser to track visited pages.
5. Select OK to close the **Internet Options** dialog box.

Internet Explorer 7 Settings

To set the number of days for the history file, do this:

1. If the menu bar is not visible, right-click anywhere on the toolbar and select **Classic Menu** from the pull-down menu.
2. From the menu bar, choose **Tools**.
3. Select **Internet Options...** from the pull-down menu to open the **Internet Options – Security at Risk** dialog box.

4. Select the **General** tab.
5. In the **Browsing history** section, select **Settings** to open the **Temporary Internet Files and History Settings** dialog box.
6. In the **History** section, enter the number of days you want the browser to track visited pages.
7. Select OK to close the **Temporary Internet Files and History Settings** dialog box.
8. Select OK to close the **Internet Options** dialog box.

REVIEW THE COOKIES

A quick review of the cookies collected by your browser can also show if someone has visited a banned site. Keep in mind that a visit to one site may generate a third-party cookie, which is a cookie that is set from another site. Even though you can't tell the difference between regular and third-party cookies, all cookies can provide you with information. If a cookie is from a suspect site, it means either that site or a related site was visited.

Usually, it is easy to tell if a cookie is from a site that may have objectionable content. Often a domain name may have some relationship to the content of the associated web site. If several cookies appear to be from the same category of content, then it may indicate a pattern of behavior rather than just an accidental encounter with suspect material.

Reviewing Cookies in Firefox

To review cookies in Firefox, do the following:

1. From the menu bar, choose **Tools**.

2. Choose **Options...** from the pull-down menu to open the **Options** dialog box.
3. Select the **Privacy** tab.
4. In the **Cookies** section, select the **Show Cookies...** tab, which will open the **Cookies** dialog box.
5. From this dialog box, you can either scroll through the cookie list or use the search box to look for a particular domain name.
6. When finished, select **Close** to exit the **Cookies** dialog box, and **OK** to close the **Options** dialog box.

Reviewing Cookies in Internet Explorer 6
To review cookies, do the following:

1. From the menu bar, choose **Tools**.
2. Select **Internet Options...** from the pull-down menu to open the **Internet Options – Security at Risk** dialog box.
3. Select the **General** tab.
4. In the **Temporary Internet files** section, select **Settings...** to open the **Settings** dialog box.
5. Select the **View Files...** in order to open Windows Explorer in the directory containing the cookies.
6. Review and manage the cookies as you would any file within Windows Explorer.
7. Close Windows Explorer.
8. Select OK to close the **Settings** dialog box.
9. Select OK to close the **Internet Options** dialog box.

Reviewing Cookies in Internet Explorer 7
To review cookies, do the following:

1. From the menu bar, choose **Tools**.
2. Select **Internet Options…** from the pull-down menu to open the **Internet Options – Security at Risk** dialog box.
3. Select the **General** tab.
4. In the **Browsing history** section, select **Settings** to open the **Temporary Internet Files and History Settings** dialog box.
5. Select **View Trusted Files…** to open the Windows Explorer file management program and view the directory containing the cookies.
6. Review and manage the cookies.
7. Close Windows Explorer.
8. Select **OK** to close the **Temporary Internet Files and History Settings** dialog box.
9. Select **OK** to close the **Internet Options** dialog box.
10. Select OK to close the **Settings** dialog box.
11. Select OK to close the **Internet Options** dialog box.

STEP 7: CHECK YOUR COMPUTER'S HARD DRIVE

If you believe inappropriate content has been saved in your computer, you can search the hard drive for any offending files. The Windows Explorer file management program allows you to search for files by file type, file size, file name, and you can even search for particular words and phrases in a file. Perhaps the easiest kinds of files to find are video files, graphics files, and very large files. For graphics or video files, search for file names ending in ".jpg," ".gif," ".bmp," ".avi," ".mov," ".wmv," and ".mpg." When it comes to size, start looking for files larger than one megabyte. Increasing the file size will produce fewer files, and decreasing the limit will increase the number of files.

Additional Software for Searching Your Hard Drive
A free program that makes searching your hard drive easier is Google Desktop. It allows you to search your hard drive the way you do an online search. See appendix 1 for details on this program.

TOP 10 TIPS ABOUT INAPPROPRIATE CONTENT

1. Your family should have very clear rules about what is allowed and what is not allowed.
2. Your family rules should apply at home and away from home.
3. Inappropriate content may be sent to a family member or a family member may look for it.
4. Anyone can accidentally encounter inappropriate content online or in an email.
5. Following this book's suggestions for dealing with unwanted email and for doing online searches can help prevent accidental exposure.
6. You can use filters on your home computer to limit the kind of content that can be displayed.
7. You may also be able to use a filter in an online service such as a search engine.
8. Inappropriate content can be in an email, on a web site, on a hard drive, or stored offline.
9. Inappropriate content can be in any format, including text, graphics, or video.
10. Evidence of inappropriate activities can be in a browser's history or cookie file, in an online account, on a hard drive, or stored offline.

CHAPTER 12

ONLINE AT SCHOOL AND THE LIBRARY

In This Chapter
- Schools and the Internet
- Q&A About Being Online at School
- Top 10 Tips for Being Online at School
- Libraries and the Internet
- Q&A About Being Online at the Library
- Top 10 Tips for Being Online at the Library

The average child can go online at home, at the home of a friend or relative, at school, and at the library. Most of this book has been about what you can do to manage your child's Internet use at home, and most of this advice will also work managing Internet use at the home of a friend or a relative. This chapter will give you an idea about what happens at school or at the library. Your child needs your consent to go online in these places, but he will be under the supervision of other people. As a parent, you need to know a little about how the Internet works at school and at the library so you can make decisions that are in the best interests of your child.

Schools and the Internet

For most public and private schools, the Internet is part of the regular school experience. It could be a major part of a child's experience if your child is issued a laptop and required to use it for most classes, or there may be very limited use of the Internet during class or after school. No matter how much or how little the school uses the Internet, the following will very likely be true:

- A parent has to agree to allow a child to use the Internet at school.
- The school will have rules and codes of conduct that the students must follow.
- There will be very little formal training provided for parents or students on how to use the Internet.

This book addresses the third point, and will likely go well beyond any training the school will provide for you or your child. You should also get to know about the rules at school and be willing to get involved if you feel that the school is not doing right by your child.

Common School Rules on Internet Use

An Internet acceptable use policy is a set of rules or guidelines for how that resource may be used. Typical acceptable use polices for a school include the following:

- A list of acceptable uses of the Internet.
- A list of possible penalties for violations of the terms of the acceptable use agreement.
- A list of unacceptable uses of the Internet. This list would typically include things like sending or

forwarding abusive or threatening messages, or altering information without permission.
- A statement that the school is not responsible for any problems or losses the users may have.
- A statement that users should not expect any privacy when it comes to email and other online communications.
- A statement to be signed by both the student and a parent or guardian indicating that the agreement was read and understood.

Q&A ABOUT BEING ONLINE AT SCHOOL

Will my child have to use the Internet at school?
That will depend on the school. Some classes may require that students use the Internet to complete assignments. The school may also use the Internet to communicate with students about assignments or about administrative matters. Make sure you talk to your child or to a school official to find out about the school's policies.

Will the school's agreement cover every situation?
No set of rules can ever anticipate every possible situation. If you are aware of a situation that causes problems for your child or for other students, you may want to discuss it with your child or bring it to the attention of the school.

How will I know if my child is using the school computer to do things like look at pornography?
The school may inform parents if a child violates the school's Internet policies. You can also contact the school if you have any questions about your child's activities.

Will my child be able to use the school's computer to send personal messages?
Your child may be able to send personal messages, but because there is no guarantee of privacy when a student uses the school's computers, you may want to encourage your child to avoid the school's computer system when sending or receiving a sensitive private message.

Should my child take a laptop to school to take notes and to do assignments?
Unless the school requires the use of laptops, do not let your child take one to school. At best, it will be an inconvenience, since your child will have to carry a laptop as well as all required books and materials. Also, unless the school has wireless access, it will be difficult to use the computer to access the Internet.

What if my child needs to go online, but we don't have a computer at home?
You may be able to make arrangements with your child's school to get the online access your child needs. That could mean using the school's computer system after hours or using the computers at a public library.

I have a computer at home that does not connect to the Internet. How can my child use it for school?
Your computer probably has the basic kinds of word processing, spreadsheet, or presentation programs your child may need to write a paper or complete a project. Your child can do the work on the home computer and use a portable storage device like a flash drive to transfer work between home and school.

Top 10 Tips for Being Online at School

1. **Become familiar with school policies**: Ideally, these policies should be written and available for students and parents to review.
2. **Assume that the school can review anything your child does online**: Normally, a school has the right to review any activity that involves the school's computer system.
3. **Report any visit to an inappropriate site**: Report any cases of being sent inappropriate material or any accidental visit to an inappropriate site.
4. **Report any suspicious or unusual activity**: Make sure the school is aware of anything out of the ordinary involving the school's computer system.
5. **Don't do anything online that is against school rules**: Assume activities that are not allowed in school are also not allowed online at school.
6. **Stick to schoolwork**: Don't use the school's computers for activities unrelated to schoolwork.
7. **Make backup copies of key files** Keep backups somewhere outside the school's computer system.
8. **Free speech is limited**: Typically, a school has stricter limits on what students can do online compared with rules at the library.
9. **Make use of all the school's resources**: Internet access is just one educational resource available at school. Become familiar with the school library and other school resources that complement the Internet.
10. **Use common sense when you are online**: Some situations may not be covered by a school rule or policy. When in doubt, use common sense.

Libraries and the Internet

The Internet has become a major part of many libraries and is one of the more popular services for children and for adults. In most cases, there is no additional charge to use the library's computers. Even if you know nothing about the Internet, that should not stop you from going online at the library. Most libraries also offer classes or other guidance to help you and your family learn how to use the Internet.

If you or your child do not already have a library card, go out and get one today, and do the same for everyone in your family. A library card at a library with online access gives your child the following benefits:

- Access to the Internet from the library.
- Access to library resources from your home computer.
- Checking out and renewing books online.
- Using online library resources for school projects.

Libraries also offer online services that do not require a library card, such as homework assistance, searching the library catalog, or asking librarians questions by email.

The Role of the Library

According to data from the American Library Association, an organization of library professionals, there are more than on hundred thousand libraries and four hundred thousand library professionals in the United States. In recent years, the availability of online access has increased dramatically for libraries across the United States, with most large- and medium-sized library systems offering some kind of online access.

Many of the goals of the American Library Association will be reflected in the policies of your local library. Among those goals are support of First Amendment rights and promoting equal access to information services. What this means in practical terms is that libraries will allow any user of library services to access just about any online information without restrictions.

THE INTERNET AT THE LIBRARY

If you want your child to get the most out of the Internet at the library, you need to understand a few things about the library's role. Many library resources are available online, and a librarian can help you or your child use the Internet to find and use resources from other libraries or from elsewhere online. It is up to you as a parent to make sure your child uses these resources wisely and well.

While libraries may have classes on how to use the Internet, those classes will probably cover only part of what this book covers, most likely the kind of material contained in the chapters on how to use the Web and email. Make sure that your child is aware of the basics before going online at the library. If your child is new to the Internet or uncomfortable around strangers, you should be nearby when he goes online.

LIBRARY RULES AND THE INTERNET

The rules of conduct in a public library are mostly the same whether you are using the Internet or not. So long as you or your child are not disturbing other users in the library and respecting their rights, you have the freedom do what you please. There are additional rules for online activity by children. US federal laws, in particular the Child Internet Protection Act, affect library systems that accept federal funding. In these library systems, typically all computers in children's areas of the library are only allowed filtered Internet access.

While computers in designated children's areas of libraries may have restrictions, libraries may allow parents to have restrictions on a child's online access removed for computers in other parts of the library. At least one library system allows minors to remove filtering without parental permission. The King County Library system of the state of Washington requires anyone under 17 to have filtered access to library computers, but allows anyone who is at least 17 the option of requesting unfiltered access. Each library system may have different rules about filtering Internet access, so be sure to ask your librarian for details.

THE ROLE OF A LIBRARIAN
Librarians can help you find and check out books and help you look up information, but they can do much more. You and your child should understand what a librarian can do for you, as well as what you should be doing to get the most out of the library experience.

What a Librarian Can Do for You
Librarians can be of great help in the following areas:

- Finding resources within the library, including reference information such as encyclopedias.
- Finding resources elsewhere in the library system.
- Finding the key resources in a specific area.
- Finding resources for answering specific questions.

What You or Your Child Should be Doing

To get the most out of a library, you and your child should:

- Find out what you can do online.
- Find out what resources can help with schoolwork.
- Learn how to ask a librarian the right questions.

The first point is easy; just go to the library and log on. If you have not yet been online at the library, find out how to get access on your next visit. The last two points are a little more complicated, but the following section should give you or your child the confidence to ask a librarian a question.

HOW TO USE A LIBRARIAN

Most library patrons know how to locate or check out books from library. However, you or your child will need to know more if you want him to use all that the library has to offer. On your next visit, meet with a library professional to discuss what services are available.

For questions that require a quick answer from a reference source, a librarian can help identify the best resource. If the task is more complicated, like doing research for a school project, you or your child needs to do the following before approaching a librarian:

- Take the time to understand what you need.
- Ask for help on a specific question or problem.
- Tell the librarian why you need the information and how it will be used.
- Tell the librarian what you already know.

- Ask the librarian to point out any resources that might help you.

None of the above points have anything to do with the Internet. That is because at the library, the Internet is just one of the tools that you and your child can use to find information.

Q&A About Being Online at the Library

Will my child's library have Internet filters?
While US federal laws and regulations may require filtered access for computers in the children's area of the library, different libraries interpret the rules differently for filtering elsewhere in the library. Check with your library to see what the requirements are and what options you and your children may have for filtering.

Can I ask the librarian to check on what sites my child visited while at the library?
Probably not. Many libraries delete information about a patron's computer usage after a patron logs out. Even if the data was not deleted, libraries are very protective of every patron's privacy and will likely not agree to this kind of request.

Can people watch pornography at the library?
In most libraries, yes. Many libraries in the United States permit anyone who is allowed to have unfiltered Internet access to view anything online that is legal. That includes most sexually explicit material.

If I see someone watching pornography on one of the library computers, can I tell that person to stop?
Unless that person is causing a disturbance, such as making noise or bothering other people, the library staff will probably not ask that person to stop. You may ask your librarian if there are other options available, such as moving you to another computer or perhaps putting a privacy screen on the other patron's computer.

How long can I be online on a library computer?
That depends on the library. Most libraries limit computer use to about an hour per day. If the library has wireless access, you may be able to have unlimited time online if you have a laptop with wireless capability.

Can I ask the librarian to watch my child and to prevent him from seeing objectionable things online?
The librarian is not responsible for what your child does online. It is your responsibility as a parent to oversee what your child does online. If you are not able to do this, then your child should not be online at the library.

Are there computers at the library that block pornography and other inappropriate material?
Libraries sometimes arrange computers so that those in the children's area are all filtered. Check with your library to see which computers are always filtered and which ones are not.

Can my child do school work on library computers?
Library computers often have the basic kinds of software students need to write reports and presentations. Check with your librarian to see what is available.

Top 10 Tips for Being Online at the Library

1. **Get a library card**: You will need a library card to go online at the library. If you use more than one library system, get a card for each of them.
2. **Supervise your child at the library**: The librarian is not there to look after your child. If your child needs an adult nearby, that person should be you.
3. **Check the filters on your accounts**: Make sure your child has appropriate filters for his library account.
4. **Leave other users alone**: Free speech means other library visitors can do whatever they want online, so long they are not breaking the library's rules or bothering others.
5. **Don't let other people bother you**: If someone interferes with what you are doing online, contact a staff person immediately.
6. **Make visiting the library a regular habit**: This should be the case even if there is not a single computer in the building.
7. **Learn how to work with a librarian**: Make sure you and your child are comfortable with going to a librarian to ask questions.
8. **Learn how to work with a librarian online**: This will allow your child to easily access more library resources.
9. **Make use of all the library's resources**: Make sure you and your child know about all the other resources the library may offer.
10. **Check out other library web sites**: Many library systems have online information and services that are available to the public.

Chapter 13

Beyond Email and the Web

In This Chapter
- Instant Messaging
- Chat Rooms
- Social Networking
- Blogs
- Online Videos
- Photo Sharing
- File Sharing
- Webcams
- Podcasting

The Internet is more than just email and the Web. This book has discussed online privacy, online security, email, and the Web in detail because these four areas are at the heart of your family's online experience. If you make the effort to understand these four areas, understanding how to use other popular online services and technologies will not be a problem for you or your children.

This chapter will review several of the services and technologies that are popular with children and teenagers, and will recommend what you and your children can do to safely participate in these activities.

Keep in mind that many online applications perform several functions. For example, the same online service may allow users to use instant messaging, create a blog, or run a webcam. Make sure you understand the full capabilities of any online service your child uses.

THINGS YOU SHOULD ALWAYS DO
No matter what your child does online, you should have the ability to check on what she is doing. Following are things you should do for each account or service your child uses:

- **Write down key information**: Make sure that you have written down any user names, passwords, or other information needed to access the account.
- **Become a registered user**: A registered user goes through some kind of registration process in order to use an online service. As a registered user, you can see how the service works, and what parts of it you want your child to avoid. Do this with your child so she can explain how she uses the service.
- **Review the rules of the service**: Make sure that your child is observing the rules of the service. If your child does not meet a requirement, for example, being at least as old as the minimum age limit, then she should not use the service.
- **Review your child's user profile**: Follow the suggestions in chapter 4 on privacy; that is, leave as much information blank as you can. If you have to submit something, use her online alias.
- **Set rules for each service**: As you become familiar with how a service works and how your child uses

it, devise sensible rules for her to follow while using that service.

INSTANT MESSAGING

Also know as IM, this is an Internet-based application that allows almost instant written communication among two or more individuals.

INSTANT MESSAGING BASICS

There are a few things you should know about IM before you decide if you want it on your home computer:

- **Hardware**: You do not need more hardware.
- **Software**: You'll need to add software. Four of the more popular options are AOL Instant Messenger, Yahoo! Messenger, Windows Live Messenger, and Skype. See appendix 1 for details.
- **Registration**: You have to be a registered user.
- **Cost**: Free.
- **Limitations**: If you want to IM someone, that person has to have compatible IM software. Also, users can put limits on who may send messages.

INSTANT MESSAGING ISSUES

There are several issues that parents should consider before allowing children to use IM.

PRIVACY ISSUES

Typically, you need to use a screen name. Follow the suggestions given in chapter 4 and make sure screen names do not provide any hints as to your child's name, gender, age, school, or other information that could attract unwanted attention.

CYBERBULLIES AND CHILD PREDATORS

Instant messaging can be a much more personal kind of communication than email, and may be the preferred method of some cyberbullies for intimidating your child. Also, child predators may use IM to evaluate potential victims, taking advantage of the instant feedback of IM to get your child to reveal personal information or to arrange a meeting.

RECOMMENDATIONS FOR PARENTS

Instant messaging can be a safe and useful application if you do the following:

- **Review the list of contacts**: Make sure you know who talks to your child using IM. Block anyone whom you do not want to contact your child.
- **Review past messages**: Make sure conversations are appropriate or are with people who are known to you or to your child. If you are unable to review past messages, do not allow your child to use that program.
- **Schools and Libraries**: Both libraries and schools typically will not allow users to add the additional software needed to use IM.

Keep in mind that your child may be using several instant messaging programs, so be sure to follow these steps for every IM account.

CHAT ROOMS

These are online resources that allow two or more users to type messages that can be viewed almost instantly by other active users. The conversation is usually text based, and ongoing conversations are accessible to everyone in the chat room, even those who are not typing messages.

CHAT ROOM BASICS

Communication using chat rooms is very similar to the way users communicate using IM. Messages are short, and there is near instant feedback.

- **Hardware**: You do not need more hardware.
- **Software**: Some chat rooms are available online. Others need additional software. For example, many IM programs include a chat room option.
- **Registration**: You have to be a registered user.
- **Cost**: Free.
- **Limitations**: For most chat rooms, there are no limits on who may be involved, and a conversation can include language and subjects not appropriate for children.
- **Schools and Libraries**: Most schools would not allow students to visit chat rooms, and libraries may block chat room sites for a child's account.

CHAT ROOM ISSUES

Chat rooms have the privacy issues mentioned for instant messaging. An additional issue is that of lurkers; these are people who visit a chat room to read what other people type, but who remain anonymous by not posting any of their own messages. A lurker who means harm may join the conversation only after identifying a potential victim.

RECOMMENDATIONS FOR PARENTS

Do not let any child use a chat room unless that child is under close supervision by you or another responsible person. If you are going to allow chat room visits, you may want to take the following precautions:

- **Only allow visits to moderated chat rooms**: These managed chat rooms are supposed to be focused on a particular subject, and you should make sure that the moderator is able to keep the room under control.
- **Review conversations**: If you don't have the ability to review past conversations, you may not want your child to use that chat room.

SOCIAL NETWORKING

This term is applied to online services that encourage personal or group interaction by allowing users to easily publish and exchange information about themselves and to build online profiles of themselves in order to attract people with similar interests. The most well-known social networking site is MySpace, but there are many others.

SOCIAL NETWORKING BASICS

Social networking sites allow users to create customized web pages that feature that user. The goal of many users is to invite other users of that same social networking site to become part of their online circle of friends. While anyone can view someone's social networking page, you have to be a regular user to do things such as search for a profile or send a message to another user. Some of the other things you may want to know include the following:

- **Hardware**: You do not need more hardware.
- **Software**: You do not need more software.
- **Registration**: You have to be a registered user.

Chapter 13—Beyond Email and the Web 195

- **Cost**: Free.
- **Limitations**: Many social networking sites have minimum age limits. For MySpace, that limit is 14.
- **Schools and Libraries**: Most schools restrict visits to these kinds of sites. Public libraries typically block social networking sites for a child's account.

SOCIAL NETWORKING ISSUES
The biggest issue with social networking sites is privacy. These sites encourage users to post as much personal and private information as they want.

RECOMMENDATIONS FOR PARENTS
If your child is going to use a social networking site, there are several precautions you can take:

- **Review your child's public profile**: Make sure the profile has no sensitive personal information such as photos, school, or phone number. Instead of his real name, your child should use his online alias. Also, remove anything that you do not want the rest of the world to see.
- **Review your child's list of contacts**: Make sure that you know the people your child has invited to be part of his or her network and that they have a relationship with him outside of the Internet.

BLOGS
A blog, which is short for Web log, is an online personal journal or diary. It may be on a dedicated web site or part of another site. A blog can have a combination of text, pictures, audio, or video. Because blogs are personal, the rules for what can be in a blog are up to the blog's creator.

Blog Basics

You do not need additional resources to create blogs:

- **Hardware**: You do not need more hardware.
- **Software**: You do not need more software.
- **Registration**: You have to be a registered user.
- **Cost**: Free.
- **Limitations**: Most blogging sites have few limits on what can be put online.
- **Schools and Libraries**: Libraries would likely have no restrictions, and schools may allow a visit to a blog if it is related to schoolwork. Schools may also allow students to update blogs.

Blogging Issues

Because blogs are often about the writer's personal life, you should take the time to review the content of any blog made by your child.

Privacy

Your child should not to reveal anyone's personal and private information in the blog. A person reading the blog should not be able to identify or locate any person mentioned in the blog.

Libel and Defamation

To avoid the kind of defamation-related issues described in chapter 6, encourage your child not to say anything bad about anyone online.

School-related Issues

Your child should be very careful about saying anything on a blog about teachers, students, or staff. Even if what he says is true, he may face complaints or disciplinary procedures at school.

RECOMMENDATIONS FOR PARENTS
Take the time to read your child's blog and talk to him about any part of the blog that concerns you.

ONLINE VIDEOS

Watching videos online has become a popular activity, with videos available at a number of sites. The same sites may also allow users to upload and share videos. While this is a relatively new activity, it is very likely that your child or someone she knows is either watching or creating online videos.

ONLINE VIDEO BASICS
Watching a video is as easy as clicking on a link on a web page. Most of the software you need to play videos is either already installed on your computer or free software can be found online.

- **Hardware**: You do not need more hardware.
- **Software**: You may need to add more software, and several options are freely available online.
- **Registration**: You may have to be a registered user to upload videos or access restricted content.
- **Cost**: Most content is freely available.
- **Limitations**: Uploading or downloading video files may slow down the response of other computers on a home wireless network.
- **Schools and Libraries**: Schools may not allow videos that are not related to schoolwork. Public libraries may block video sites based on content.

Online Video Issues

The most important issue for parents is the content of the videos. Some video sites have restrictions on content, and other sites may allow any kind of content.

Recommendations for Parents

If your child is going to view videos online, there are several precautions you can take:

- **Review the site's policies**: If a site allows explicit sexual content, you may want to add a family rule that makes that site off-limits. You may also want to use any available filtering on your home computer or within the web site to limit what can be seen or downloaded.
- **Find videos you want to watch**: Because such a wide variety videos are online, there are probably many that will be interesting to you and your child.

Photo Sharing

This is an online service that allows users to upload, organize, and distribute photos. The photos may either be available to anyone online, or restricted to invited guests.

Photo Sharing Basics

Photo sharing is done through an online provider, and you may need additional resources to make it happen:

- **Hardware**: You do not need more hardware.
- **Software**: No additional software is required to view photos online. Additional software may be required for uploading photos.

- **Registration**: Only registered users can upload photos.
- **Cost**: Free.
- **Limitations**: The service provider may limit the kind of material that can be placed online.
- **Schools and Libraries**: Photo sharing sites may be filtered or blocked.

PHOTO SHARING ISSUES

The biggest potential problem is privacy. Do not permit any photo to be placed online that will allow anyone to identify or locate your child or your home. Also, you or your child should get permission before placing a photo of someone online if that person can be identified in the photo.

RECOMMENDATIONS FOR PARENTS

Approve any photos your child wants to put online and remove any that you think are inappropriate.

FILE SHARING

File sharing, sometimes called peer-to-peer file sharing, is the process of using the Internet to transfer files directly from one personal computer to another. This is different from downloading a file from a web site because the files are not coming from servers on the Internet, but rather from users who are connected to the Internet.

FILE SHARING BASICS

In order to do file sharing, your personal computer has to have software dedicated for that purpose.

File Sharing Issues

Because most file sharing software allows files to be downloaded from other personal computers, the risk from malicious software is quite high. If the software is not set up properly, you could mistakenly allow other people to copy files you don't mean to share, or you could be sent material that you do not want on your computer.

Recommendations for Parents

Because the risks are so great and because there are other options for transferring files between computers, you should not allow your children to use file sharing software. If there is a file sharing program on your family's computer, it should be removed.

Webcams

A webcam is simply a digital camera that is connected to a computer and that can be used to send live images to a web site, chat room, or some other part of the Internet. The typical webcam on a home computer is set up to take pictures of the person at the keyboard.

Webcam Basics

Webcams are digital cameras designed to upload images to the Internet. You will need the following to use a webcam:

- **Hardware**: Other than the webcam, you will not need additional hardware.
- **Software**: If you need more software, it will be included with a new webcam.
- **Registration**: You may need to register with an online service to transmit webcam images.

- **Cost**: Prices can start from less than $20.
- **Limitations**: The webcam must be connected to the computer.
- **Schools and Libraries**: It is unlikely that schools or libraries would allow webcams on their computers.

WEBCAM ISSUES

Using webcams can lead to serious privacy and security issues. They are typically set up to broadcast images of whoever is sitting in front of the computer, so anyone looking at the video will know that person's gender and approximate age, two facts that most online predators want to know. If someone, especially a stranger, encourages your child to use a webcam or sends one as a gift, you should not allow it. This kind of request is a common tactic used by online child predators.

RECOMMENDATIONS FOR PARENTS

To protect your family's privacy and security, take the following precautions:

- **Only use webcams offline**: Do not allow your child to broadcast live images to the Internet.
- **Limit the use of the webcam**: When the webcam is not in use, turn it off or cover the lens.

PODCASTING

A podcast is an audio or video file distributed using the Internet. Based on a combination of the words *iPod* and *broadcast*, podcasting is not limited to iPods, but can involve any technology that allows audio or visual files to be distributed online and played on computers or other electronic devices.

Podcasting Basics

These files can be either played immediately or saved for later playback. Freely available software makes it easy to create basic audio or video podcasts. Some services allow anyone to upload and distribute podcasts online.

Some of things you need to do or items you need to create or enjoy podcasts include the following:

- **Hardware**: You may need to get a microphone for creating your audio podcast or a microphone and a video camera to create a video podcast.
- **Software**: You may want to add software to make it easier to create podcasts, or to organize, play, or download, podcasts. Appendix 1 lists several of these free programs.
- **Registration**: You have to be a registered user to upload podcasts or to subscribe to podcasts.
- **Cost**: Many podcasts are free, but some commercial podcasts are not free.
- **Limitations**: Some services that distribute podcasts may have age limits due to content.
- **Schools and Libraries**: Some podcast sites may be restricted by a school or a library due to content. Also, public library computers may not allow users to download files, including podcast files.

Podcasting Issues

The biggest issue with downloading podcasts is with content. You often have no idea if a podcast contains objectionable material until it is played. Enjoying podcasts is a lot easier if you do the following:

- **Organize your podcasts**: Find free software, such as the iTunes media player, that allows you to both play and organize podcasts. You do not need an iPod to use iTunes. The software allows you to limit the kinds of content that can be downloaded.
- **Review your child's downloads**: Only allow your child to download a podcast after getting your permission. Also, review the podcasts to make sure the content is acceptable.

If your child is thinking about creating podcasts, she can do the following and start without spending any money:

- **Do some research**: You and your child can go online or to the library to learn how to make podcasts or to find examples of podcasts.
- **Get some editing software**: A free tool for editing audio is Audacity (see appendix 1). Windows XP also comes with the Windows Movie Maker video editing program.
- **Start without extra equipment**: Before spending any money, practice using the audio or video files on your computer or ones you may find online.
- **Have a plan**: If your child wants to create an audio or video podcast, make sure that she is motivated to do so and has some idea of what it takes to make it happen.

Creating Low-Budget Podcasts

Creating a podcast does not have to be complicated, difficult or expensive. That certainly was the case when I created my first podcast series *The Conversation at AirSafe.com*. Knowing almost nothing about podcasts, I made use of search engines and public libraries to find enough information to get started. Within a month, I had gone from knowing very little about the process to creating a podcast series and getting it listed on iTunes. I did not need to add any computer hardware, and the additional software I needed was free. The total cost of a book on podcasting, a microphone, and other audio-related hardware was about $100. For the *Parenting and the Internet* podcast, I already had all the resources I needed, so I did not have to spend any more money. If you or your child want to know more about how to create a podcast, visit the *Parenting and the Internet* podcast at http://podcast.speedbrake.com, or the home page of *The Conversation at AirSafe.com* podcast at http://podcast.airsafe.org.

Chapter 14

Managing the Internet

In This Chapter
- Setting Up Your Notebook
- Setting the Ground Rules
- Setting Up Your Home Computer
- Family Privacy Review
- Family Security Review
- Review of Online Basics
- Things You Should Do Regularly
- The Stuff at the Back of the Book

Managing your family's online activities does not have to take a lot of time or be complicated. A little planning and preparation makes this process a lot easier.

Setting Up Your Notebook

Your first management task is to set up a notebook to keep track of paperwork. A basic three-ring notebook with a few dividers should do just fine. Create a separate section for each family member and one for shared resources. The following forms, as well as the sample Internet use agreements in appendix 3, are all located in the Family Forms Pack at http://forms.speedbrake.com:

- **Ground Rules for Using the Computer and for Being Online**: You'll find several suggested rules in the next section. Feel free to add, delete, or edit the rules on that list.
- **List of Online Activities**: Use this form to describe the activity or service, as well as any information needed to participate in the activity or the service.
- **List of Additional Software**: Each of your family's computers should have its own list.
- **List of Data Storage Devices**: Use this form to track each family member's data storage devices, as well as for shared storage devices.

SETTING THE GROUND RULES

This is an activity that will evolve. As you become more familiar with how you and your child use the computer, you will come up with new rules regarding what your child is allowed to do online. Rules that best fit the philosophy of this book are listed below and are also available in the Family Forms Pack:

1. Parents make the rules when it comes to using the computer and the Internet.
2. Parents should respect a child's privacy, but should also be able to look at any file or get into any account at any time. This means that parents should know every password, user name, or screen name their child uses.
3. Parents must approve of any software before it is added to any computer at home.
4. The rules that apply at home also apply away from home.

5. Using the computer or being online is a privilege, not a right.
6. Protect your personal privacy online, as well as the privacy of others.
7. Do your best to stay safe online.
8. Everyone should help one another learn about computers and the Internet.
9. Don't do anything online that you want to keep a secret or that will embarrass you if made public.
10. If something unexpected or scary happens while you are online or on the computer, tell someone.

SETTING UP YOUR HOME COMPUTER

Chapter 3 discussed the basic hardware and software you will need, and chapters 4 and 5 have details on how to set up your system to keep uninvited software and uninvited people away from your computer. You should also refer to any setup instructions provided by the manufacturer.

WIRELESS SECURITY

If you are using a wireless network at home, set up your system so you can protect your network from most intruders. If you have any questions about setting up the security, check your documentation or contact your ISP.

COMPUTER SECURITY

It is important that you have basic security protections in place before you go online or immediately after you go online. If your ISP provides protection, you will likely have to go online first. If you are providing your own security software, then make sure it is set up before you go online. Refer to your documentation to ensure you are setting things up correctly.

Family Privacy Review

Chapter 4 went into detail about how to protect your family's online privacy in the "Seven Steps to Online Privacy" section. Follow those steps either on a regular schedule or whenever you suspect a privacy problem with your family's online activities.

Family Security Review

Chapter 5 went into detail about improving your online security in the "Seven Steps to Online Security" section. Follow those steps either on a regular schedule or whenever you suspect a privacy problem with your family's online activities.

Because of the close relationship between online privacy and online security, you should perform privacy reviews the same time you perform security reviews.

Review of the Online Basics

Chapters 6 through 13 covered several key online issues that you and your child should understand. If you have questions or problems in the following areas, review the appropriate chapter:

- Chapter 6: Internet Legal and Ethical Issues.
- Chapter 7: Cyberbullies and Child Predators.
- Chapter 8: Email Basics.
- Chapter 9: Dealing with Unwanted Email.
- Chapter10: Web Basics.
- Chapter 11: Avoiding Inappropriate Content.
- Chapter 12: Schools, Libraries, and the Internet.
- Chapter 13: Beyond Email and the Web.

THINGS YOU SHOULD DO REGULARLY

Once you have set up your computer and you and your child have had time to get some online experience, you should take time regularly to see how things are going. While the following list does not include everything that you can do to keep up with your online child, taking these actions can often stop problems when they are still small:

- Any time you see your child doing something unusual on the computer, make sure it is an activity on the "List of Online Activities."
- Regularly review your family's online activities as described in the "Seven Steps" procedures from chapter 4 (privacy), chapter 5 (security), chapter 9 (email), and chapter 11 (inappropriate content).

THE STUFF AT THE BACK OF THE BOOK

The sections at the back of the book are full of information that will be useful to you and your child.

APPENDIX 1—RECOMMENDED FREE SOFTWARE

These programs are not only free, but also very useful. The software in this section can turn even a basic computer into a very powerful tool.

APPENDIX 2—RECOMMENDED ONLINE RESOURCES

What makes the Internet such a powerful tool is that it's very easy for you and your child to connect with free online resources that provide solid information for school or for entertainment.

APPENDIX 3—INTERNET USE AGREEMENTS

These sample use agreements can be used as models for the ones you can create for your family.

GLOSSARY

This section will give you a basic explanation of many of the concepts, technologies, and online services mentioned in this book.

Appendix 1

Free Software

In This Appendix
- Web Browsers
- Business and Office Software
- Communications Software
- Security-related Software
- Media Software
- Email Programs
- Hard Drive Search Software
- Geography Reference Software

All the software applications in this section have one thing in common—all of them can be used for free. The Microsoft-related software products in this appendix are either included with the Windows XP or Windows Vista operating system, or they can be downloaded from the Microsoft web site. The other programs featured here can be found at the URLs that are included with the descriptions.

Risks of From Software
Any time that you add software to your computer, you want to avoid problems either with the software or with your computer, especially from viruses, spyware, and

other malicious software. While it is possible that the free software that you download could have problems, you can avoid many potential issues by taking the following precautions:

- **Look for reviews of the software**: Two excellent resources for finding reviews of free software are Sourceforge.net at http://sourceforge.net and Download.com at http://www.download.com. You can also find comparisons with similar software and find out additional information such as how frequently a program has been updated or downloaded.
- **Trust your instincts**: If there is anything about a program or the maker of the program that arouse your suspicions, don't download the software.
- **Use trusted software makers**: Many free programs available online were created by established software companies or nonprofit organizations. Many of these software makers also provide updates, documentation, and technical support.

> **WARNING**: If your computer is infected with spyware, adware, or other malicious software, it may direct you to somewhere other than the links listed below. If this happens, do not download any software, or take any other actions on that site. If you have an antivirus or antispyware program on your computer, use it to check your computer for malicious software. If you suspect that your computer is infected, you can also visit these sites using a computer that is not infected.

Web Browsers

**Internet Explorer—
Included in Windows XP and Windows Vista**
This browser is the most widely used; most web sites are compatible with it. For more information, visit the Internet Explorer site at http://www.microsoft.com/windows/ie/.

Firefox—http://www.mozilla.com/firefox/
This is the second most popular browser behind Internet Explorer. It is designed to aggressively block viruses, spyware, and popup ads. More features that can be added to the browser by using free downloads available on the Firefox site.

Business and Office Software

Notepad—Included in Windows XP and Windows Vista
This text editor has no spell checker or other advanced features common to most word processing programs. This program can be accessed at **Start> All Programs> Accessories> Notepad**.

WordPad—Included in Windows XP and Windows Vista
This is a basic word processor that allows users to format text and graphics, but has no spell checker or other advanced word processing features. This program can be accessed at **Start>All Programs> Accessories> WordPad**.

OpenOffice.org—http://www.openoffice.org
This office application suite includes a word processor, database manager, and presentation manager. These programs can read and work with files from a number of similar programs.

Adobe Reader — http://www.adobe.com/downloads/
This software can be used to view, print, and search PDF files. Many of the supplemental documents associated with this book are available in PDF format at http://forms.speedbrake.com.

COMMUNICATIONS SOFTWARE

Skype — http://www.skype.com
This software is primarily designed for voice communication, but it also allows text-based instant messaging as well as a video connection with other Skype users.

Windows Live Messenger — http://get.live.com/messenger/overview/
This successor to MSN Messenger allows multiple types of communication, including instant messaging, sending and receiving files, as well as voice and video chat. Also, users of Windows Live Messenger communicate with Yahoo! Instant Messenger users.

AOL Instant Messenger — http://www.aim.com
This IM program offers text based instant messaging as well as voice and video chat.

Yahoo! Instant Messenger — http://messenger.yahoo.com
This software allows text-based instant messaging, voice chat, and the ability to share files of up to one gigabyte with other users. Yahoo! Instant Messenger users can also communicate with users of Windows Live Messenger.

SECURITY-RELATED SOFTWARE

AVG Antivirus — http://www.grisoft.com
This antivirus software provides real-time antivirus protection for files and emails.

Appendix 1—Free Software

Zone Alarm — http://www.zonelabs.com
This basic firewall identifies and blocks hackers and malicious software from invading your computer.

Ad-Aware SE Personal — http://www.lavasoft.com/software/adaware/
This antispyware product provides basic protection against spyware and helps to protect your private data.

Comodo Firewall — http://www.personalfirewall.comodo.com
This firewall program allows the user to control what programs can have Internet access from your computer.

Comodo i-Vault — http://www.comodogroup.com/products/i-vault/
This automated password manager can also generate complex passwords that can enhance your security.

McAfee Site Advisor — http://www.siteadvisor.com
This plug-in for Internet Explorer and Firefox evaluates web sites for dangerous downloads and other problems.

Microsoft Malicious Software Removal Tool — http://www.microsoft.com/security/malwareremove/
This software scans computers running the Windows XP or Windows 2000 operating systems for malicious software.

Windows Defender — http://www.windowsdefender.com
This Microsoft program helps protect your computer against popups, slow performance, and security threats caused by spyware and other malicious or unwanted software. It also recommends actions a user can take when spyware programs are detected.

Media Software

iTunes – http:/www.apple.com/itunes/download/
This media player and organizer allows you to play and manage video and audio files from several formats. It can also be used to download podcasts or to create audio CDs from material in your media collection. This application also has parental control options.

Audacity – http://audacity.sourceforge.net
This audio recording and editing software package can be used to produce podcasts or to edit one or more sources of audio information. You can also export the finished files in different audio formats, including MP3.

Picasa – http://picasa.google.com
This photo organizer program allows you to edit, manage, and share the pictures and other graphics files on your computer. It can automatically locate and organize all the graphics files on your hard drive, upload visual content from external media like a digital camera or a flash drive, or save your pictures on to a CD-ROM.

QuickTime Player – http://www.apple.com/quicktime/download/
This digital media player can handle the audio and video formats used for Apple personal computers.

Real Player – http://www.real.com
This digital media player can play audio and graphics files associated with both Apple personal computers and computers that use the Windows operating system. It can act as a CD or DVD player, organize media files, and create CDs from your audio files.

Windows Media Player—
Included in Windows XP and Windows Vista
This digital media player is capable of playing several types of audio and video files, and displaying still images. You can also use this program to organize media files and create audio CDs.

Windows Movie Maker—
Included in Windows XP and Windows Vista
This video editing program is included with Windows XP Service Pack 2. and with Windows Vista. The program accepts audio and video input from several formats, and the output can be played on the Windows Media Player.

EMAIL PROGRAMS

Eurdora — http://www.eudora.com/download/
The free version of this email program includes all of the basics needed to send and receive email.

Outlook Express — Included in Internet Explorer
This program has all the basic functions of an email client program, including an address book and newsgroup access. It is also possible to create rules that can route incoming email into different folders. More information and online support is available at http://www.microsoft.com/windows/oe/.

Thunderbird — http://www.mozilla.com/thunderbird/
This email client program is from the same organization that developed the Firefox browser. Users can import existing email accounts and messages into this program. Thunderbird allows users to search messages, check the spelling of outgoing emails, and filter incoming messages.

Hard Drive Search Software

Google Desktop — http://desktop.google.com
This program allows you to perform searches your computer's hard drive in the same way that you do online searches with the Google search engine. It can find IM chats, image files, video files, audio files, spreadsheets, document files, PDF files, emails, and recently visited web pages. Unlike Google searches on the Web, no advertising appears with your search results.

Windows Desktop Search — http://toolbar.live.com
This search program from Microsoft allows you to find email messages, documents, and many other file types located on your hard drive.

Geography Reference Software

Google Earth — http://earth.google.com
This mapping software combines satellite imagery, maps, and Google search technology to allow you to view large areas of the Earth. Some areas such as large US cities have particularly detailed information.

Google SketchUp — http://sketchup.google.com
This modeling program allows you to create three-dimensional models of buildings, furniture, and other objects. The program also allows you to add a three-dimensional model of structures to the two-dimensional overhead photos used in Google Earth.

Appendix 2

Online Resources

In This Appendix
- Internet Safety and Security
- Online Parenting Resources
- Search Engines and Directories
- Copyright and Intellectual Property
- Email Accounts
- Social Networking Resources
- Computer and Internet Resources
- Dictionary and Thesaurus Resources
- Book and Library Resources
- Encyclopedias and General References
- World Geography and Politics Resources
- Financial Information Resources
- News and Weather Resources
- Homework and Study Resources
- Art and Museum Resources
- Writing and Literature Resources
- Earth and Space Resources
- Math and Science Resources
- Medical and Health Resources
- Education and Research Resources
- Audio and Video Entertainment
- Photo Sharing Resources

INTERNET SAFETY AND SECURITY

SafeKids.com — http://www.safekids.com
A family-oriented guide to making the Internet fun, safe, and productive. Contains links to informational sites and to articles on computer and Internet safety and security.

CyberTipLine — http://www.cybertipline.com
An online service that allows users to report cases of child sexual exploitation including child pornography, solicitation of children for sex acts, child molestation, and unsolicited obscene material sent to a child. Reports can be made by phone at 1-800-843-5678.

CyberWise.ca — http://cyberwise.ca
This site provides resources, information, and links for kids and teens on how to use the Internet, as well as information on how to keep children safe online.

Komando Kids — http://www.komando.com/kids/
This part of radio talk show host Kim Komando's web site provides links to many of her Internet-related articles.

US Federal Trade Commission — http://www.ftc.gov/idtheft/
This is a comprehensive resource for understanding identity theft, including how you can detect and deter such crimes, and specific actions to perform if you are a victim.

GetNetWise — http://www.getnetwise.org
This site, which is sponsored by the the Internet industry and by various public interest organizations, provides resources and advice for avoiding and minimizing Internet-related risks.

National Center for Missing and Exploited Children — http://www.missingkids.com

The mission of this nonprofit organization is to help prevent child abduction and sexual exploitation; help find missing children; and assist victims of child abduction and sexual exploitation.

Net Family News — http://netfamilynews.org

This nonprofit organization provides a forum for technology and media issues that concern children. Includes a weekly newsletter and other resources.

OnGuardOnline.gov — http://www.onguardonline.gov

This US Federal Trade Commission site provides advice on how to identify and avoid fraudulent and deceptive practices, and tips on protecting both your personal information and your computer from online threats.

McAfee Free Security Services — http://us.mcafee.com/root/catalog.asp?catid=free

This site offers a free online virus scan that will provide a list of any viruses present on your computer. Another online service evaluates the security of your wireless network.

Microsoft Windows Live OneCare — http://safety.live.com

This site provides several different kinds of online tools that can find and remove viruses and other malicious software.

NetSmartz — http://www.netsmartz.org

Operated by the National Center for Missing and Exploited Children, this site provides resources for understanding how to stay safer online.

Spyware Warrior — http://www.spywarewarrior.com

Links to spyware-related resources and online forums, as well as comparisons of antispyware products.

StaySafe.org — http://www.staysafe.org
This educational site helps consumers understand how to manage a variety of online safety and security issues, and provides how-to advice for hardware and software.

Symantec Security Check — http://security.symantec.com/ssc/
This site has three separate free online tests. The first tests your computer's vulnerability to online security risks and makes suggestions about how to make your computer more secure. The second detects viruses, and the third tracks the route taken by a potential attack.

Teenangels — http://www.teenangels.org
This site works with leading safety experts and with law enforcement organizations to train 13- to 18-year-old volunteers in all aspects of online safety, privacy, and security. These volunteers then work within their schools to promote online safety.

WiredSafety.org — http://www.wiredsafety.org
Staffed by hundreds of volunteers around the world, this site provides education, assistance, and awareness on all aspects of Internet-related crime and abuse, privacy, security, and responsible technology use.

ONLINE PARENTING RESOURCES

Childnet International — http://www.childnet-int.org
This nonprofit organization from the United Kingdom organizes a number of projects that provide useful information for both parents and children on how to use the Internet.

Chatdanger — http://www.chatdanger.com
This Childnet International site discusses the potential dangers of interactive online services such as chat, instant messaging, and online games, and also offers advice on how to engage in these activities more safely.

Kidsmart — http://www.kidsmart.org.uk
This Childnet International site provides children, parents, and teachers with information on making the Internet experience safer and more fun for children.

Sorted — http://www.childnet-int.org/sorted/
This Childnet International site provides advice on computer security issues and includes information about viruses, spyware, phishing, identity theft, and file sharing.

SuperKids — http://www.superkids.com
The site has reviews and ratings of educational software and links to online and offline educational tools.

Yahoo! Family Resource Center — http://family.yahoo.com
The site has advice for safe browsing and safe communication, as well as links to the Yahooligans! Web guide for kids.

SEARCH ENGINES AND DIRECTORIES

Ask.com — http://www.ask.com
This search engine allows users to pose search queries using questions as well as keywords and key phrases.

Ask for Kids — http://www.askforkids.com
This child friendly search site allows users to create a search request in the form of a question.

Open Directory Project — http://www.dmoz.com
Sites in this directory are screened by a team of volunteers. By selecting the *advanced* link on the home page, you can limit search results to material appropriate for children, teenagers, and mature teenagers.

Google — http://www.google.com
The most popular search engine on the Web, the site includes language translation and language specific searching. Users can change the level of filtering by selecting the *Preferences* link on the Google home page and choosing from three options: strict filtering of explicit text and images, moderate filtering of explicit images only, or no filtering at all.

KidsClick! — http://www.kidsclick.org
This directory is a project of the Ramapo Catskill Library System and is a guide to sites that are considered to be entertaining or enlightening for children.

Yahoo! Search — http://search.yahoo.com
This search engine allows users to filter search results. Users can set the level of filtering by selecting the *Advanced Search* link on the home page and then selecting the Yahoo! SafeSearch option that will filter out explicit, adult-oriented content from the search results.

Yahoo! Directory — http://dir.yahoo.com
This site has direct links to the major subject areas of the Yahoo! Directory, as well as a search function that allows you to search either the Web or the Yahoo! Directory. There are no links to filter controls on this home page, but if you set up a filtering option on the Yahoo! Search page, those settings will apply to the directory.

Yahooligans! – http://yahooligans.yahoo.com
This combination of search engine and directory will provide search results that are designed to be appropriate for children. This site also has links to numerous resources on how to safely use online resources.

Live Search – http://www.live.com
The successor to MSN search, this is the search engine used by the MSN.com site. This search engine allows users to filter search results.

Search Engine Showdown – http://searchengineshowdown.com
This site has information about changes and innovations in search engine technology, as well as comparisons of the features of many of the most popular search engines.

COPYRIGHT AND INTELLECTUAL PROPERTY

Creative Commons – http://www.creativecommons.org
Provides extensive resources that explain the concept of a Creative Commons License, how it differs from a traditional copyright, and how material with such a license may be used.

Electronic Frontier Foundation – http://www.eff.org
This nonprofit organization supports privacy, intellectual, fair use, and free speech rights on behalf of the online community.

Public Domain Music List – http://www.pdinfo.com/list.htm
A database of songs and musical works published before 1923 in the United States and that are now in the public domain.

Stanford University Library — http://fairuse.stanford.edu
This site has extensive resources on copyright issues, including the concepts of fair use of copyrighted material and material that is in the public domain.

Indiana University Copyright Management Center — http://copyright.iupui.edu
The site provides explanations of how to obtain permission to use copyrighted material, how to obtain copyright protection, and a checklist that helps to determine if a planned use of copyrighted material constitutes fair use.

United States Copyright Office — http://www.copyright.gov
Provides extensive information on copyright and fair use, and information on how to register a copyright.

United States Patent and Trademark Office — http://www.uspto.gov
Provides extensive information about trademarks and service marks, including instructions on how to register a trademark or service mark.

EMAIL ACCOUNTS

About.com — http://email.about.com
Extensive information about various email options, as well as comparisons of various free email services.

AIM Mail — http://www.aim.com
This email service from America Online can be used with AOL Instant Messenger. Users are allowed up to two gigabytes of storage.

Gmail — http://www.gmail.com
This service allows several gigabytes of storage. Messages can be forwarded to other accounts, and users can also download messages into an email program.

Windows Live Hotmail — http://hotmail.msn.com
Accounts on this Web-based email service from Microsoft have limited storage, but the limit increases once the account has been verified. Email and attachments of up to 10MB can be sent or received.

Yahoo! Mail — http://mail.yahoo.com
Mail can be sent and received online, and can also be forwarded to other accounts or download messages into an email program. Users can also retrieve mail from other accounts while within Yahoo! Mail.

SOCIAL NETWORKING RESOURCES

BlogSafety.com — http://www.blogsafety.com
The site has resources aimed at parents, teens, educators, advocates, and others who are interested in the impact of blogs, newsgroups, and other social aspects of the Web. Includes safe blogging tips for teens.

Parent's Guide to MySpace.com — http://www.parentsguidetomyspace.com
Provides detailed information on how parents can find their child's profile on MySpace.com, and how they can ensure their child does not place compromising information online and available to the general public.

COMPUTER AND INTERNET RESOURCES

Acronym Finder — http://www.acronymfinder.com
A searchable database of hundreds of thousands of acronyms and abbreviations related to computers, telecommunications, technology, and the military.

Ask Bob Rankin — http://www.askbobrankin.com
Programmer and computer technology author Bob Rankin provides easy-to-understand technical advice for a number of Internet-related subjects such as online multimedia, security, privacy, and search engines.

AskLeo! — http://ask-leo.com
A resource with links to hundreds of questions and answers about personal computers, with many detailed answers related to using Outlook Express.

ComputerHope.com — http://www.computerhope.com
A collection of free services that allows any user to access a database of extensive computer-related information, including hardware and software support for a variety of systems.

Download.com — http://www.download.com
The site has a wide range of free software for download, including security-related software. The site also has extensive tutorials and other resources that explain how to use software and how to use the Internet.

Internet101.org — http://www.internet101.org
A guide that explains the basics of the Internet in plain English. It provides a short history plus background information on several topics, including email, chat, viruses, searching, online shopping, and newsgroups.

Learn the Net.com — http://www.learnthenet.com
The site provides a basic understanding of how to set up and use a personal computer and how use various online services.

NetLingo — http://www.netlingo.com
Contains definitions to thousands of computer- and Internet-related terms. Also has explanations for many of the acronyms and slang terms that are often used in email, instant messaging, and other online communications.

Sourceforge.net — http://sourceforge.net
This site has a wide range of free software for download, and is one of the largest online resources for open source projects. These are software projects run by volunteers who work together to develop new software.

Urban Dictionary — http://www.urbandictionary.com
A user-generated dictionary of slang English words and phrases. There are approximately one million definitions, some of which are not suitable for children.

DICTIONARY AND THESAURUS RESOURCES

Dictionary.com — http://dictionary.reference.com
A multiple source dictionary search service that returns results from other online dictionaries.

Merriam — Webster Online — http://www.m-w.com
Provides links to both an online dictionary and thesaurus. For many definitions, you can also listen to the pronunciation of the word.

One Look Dictionary Search — http://www.onelook.com
A search engine that allows searches on more than five million words from more than 900 online dictionaries.

Webopedia — http://www.webopedia.com
An online dictionary and search engine for computer- and Internet-related terms.

BOOK AND LIBRARY RESOURCES

Answers.com — http://www.answers.com
This resource draws from reference works from traditional publishers and online reference sources.

Amazon.com — http://www.amazon.com
In addition to being an online bookstore, this site also has extensive information about books, including sample pages, reviews, and publisher information.

Bartleby.com — http://www.bartleby.com
A multiple reference site that has links to several sources for quotations, encyclopedias, and numerous books from the Harvard Classics series.

BUBL Information Service — http://bubl.ac.uk
This directory is hosted by Strathclide University in Scotland and uses the Dewey Decimal Classification system to catalog selected Internet resources. The directory covers all academic subject areas.

Federal Resources for Education Excellence — http://www.free.ed.gov
Site has links to more than 1,500 education resources created by numerous US federal agencies.

Appendix 2—Online Resources 231

Google Book Search — http://books.google.com
This search engine allows a user to find books using the author's name, the book's title, or even by using words and phrases that may be in the book. Some books have their entire contents available online and others may only have limited content available. A user can also find links to local libraries that may have the book in their collections.

The Internet Public Library — http://www.ipl.org
This site from the University of Michigan School of Information provides library services to Internet users. Activities include finding, evaluating, and organizing information resources.

Library of Congress Online Catalog — http://catalog.loc.gov
This search engine allows a user to find books by author, title, subject, call number, or keyword. This site also has links to the Library's photographic and audio catalogs.

Library of Congress Ask a Librarian Service — http://www.loc.gov/rr/askalib/
This site shows users how to use email, regular mail, phone, or fax to ask questions of Libary of Congress reference librarians.

Library of Congress Virtual Reference Shelf — http://www.loc.gov/rr/askalib/virtualref.html
A directory with links to dozens of different online reference sources in areas such as abbreviations, almanacs, quotations, statistics, music, and literature.

The Online Books Page — http://onlinebooks.library.upenn.edu
This resource from the University of Pennsylvania Library contains a searchable database of thousands of books that can be viewed for free online.

Project Gutenberg — http://www.gutenberg.org
This resource contains a searchable database of more than 20,000 books that can be downloaded for free.

ENCYCLOPEDIAS AND GENERAL REFERENCES

Encarta — http://encarta.msn.com
A free online version of the Microsoft reference software. Site also links to a dictionary, thesaurus, and atlas.

Encyclopedia Britannica Online — http://www.britannica.com
A search and directory site featuring *Encyclopedia Britannica*. The free online version offers a concise version of the material in the full encyclopedia.

The Free Dictionary — http://www.thefreedictionary.com
A multiple reference site that allows searches on specialized dictionaries for finance, computing, medicine, and law, as well as searches in the online *Colombia Encyclopedia*.

HowStuffWorks — http://www.howstuffworks.com
A source of unbiased, and easy-to-understand explanations of how things work. Areas covered include technology, social behaviors, and consumer products. The site also has consumer opinions and exclusive access to independent expert ratings and reviews.

Infoplease — http://www.infoplease.com
Searchable almanac, dictionary, atlas, and encyclopedia.

The Museum of Modern Art — http://www.moma.org
The site includes the museum's online collection of more than 5,000 items from several of the the museum's departments. The museum's audio programs are also available for download.

The Straight Dope — http://www.straightdope.com
A searchable database of the syndicated weekly question and answer column by Cecil Adams. The site has links to most of the columns from the past ten years and to selected columns going back to 1973.

The Urban Legends Reference Pages — http://www.snopes.com
This site is devoted to the study of contemporary lore, with an extensive collection of rumors, urban legends, and other claims that are researched and judged to be either true, false, or something in between.

US Government Manual — http://www.gpoaccess.gov/gmanual/
This is the official handbook of the federal government, and it provides information on the agencies in the legislative, judicial, and executive branches of government, as well as information on other agencies, and international organizations.

Virtual Reference Collection — http://libraries.mit.edu/help/virtualref.html
This part of the MIT Libraries site provides links to almanacs, information on corporations, data on associations, and other reference resources.

Wikipedia — http://www.wikipedia.org
This online encyclopedia is maintained by volunteers and contains entries on topics found in encyclopedias, as well as on topics typically found in almanacs and news publications. Entries may be added or removed at any time by volunteers, and may contain material that parents could find objectionable or offensive.

World Geography and Politics Resources

**Congressional Research Service (CRS) Reports —
http://www.fas.org/sgp/crs/**
This resource of the Federation of American Scientists provides a searchable database of publications from the Congressional Research Service. This congressional support agency does not make its publications directly available to the public online, but its collection provides access to many of the CRS reports that address national security, foreign policy, and related topics.

Google Maps — http://maps.google.com
This site provides detailed street maps for the area around a given address, can provide detailed travel directions, and can also show either satellite photos or satellite photos with an overlay of a street map.

**Library of Congress Portals to the World —
http://www.loc.gov/rr/international/portals.html**
Contains selective links providing authoritative, in-depth information about the nations and other areas of the world. They are arranged by country or area with the links for each sorted into a wide range of broad categories.

**Library of Congress Research Guides and Database —
http://www.loc.gov/rr/international/spguides.html**
Links to a number of specialized resources, including more than 100 online editions of the Country Study series. Each work in this series has a description and analysis of the historical setting and the social, economic, political, and national security systems and institutions of a country.

The National Geographic Society—
http://nationalgeographic.com
This site has several geography resources, including an online atlas and printable maps. It also has information about the National Geographic Bee, an academic competition for fourth to eighth grade students.

The Nuclear Information Project—
http://www.nukestrat.com
The Nuclear Information Project provides the public with access to declassified documents and analysis about nuclear weapons policy and operations, including the likely location of the nuclear warheads in the arsenal of the United States.

Perry-Castañeda Library Map Collection—
http://www.lib.utexas.edu/maps/
A collection of mostly public domain maps from the University of Texas Libraries. Includes historical and contemporary maps covering the entire world.

TopoZone—http://www.topozone.com
Online topographic maps covering the United States.

The World Factbook—
https://www.cia.gov/cia/publications/factbook/
This site is based on the reference book of the same name that is published by the US Central Intelligence Agency. The site has factual information on the political and social situations of the world's nations. Other information includes maps, natural resources, legal systems, political parties, and mortality rates. All information in the book or on the web site, except for the official seal of the CIA, is in the public domain.

WorldStatesmen.org — http://www.worldstatesmen.org
This site is a frequently updated encyclopedia of all the leaders of nations and territories. International organizations and recent religious leaders are listed separately. This site provides detailed chronologies, flags, national anthems, maps and indexes.

Chiefs of State of Foreign Governments — https://www.cia.gov/cia/publications/chiefs/
The Central Intelligence Agency publishes and updates the online directory of *Chiefs of State and Cabinet Members of Foreign Governments* weekly. The directory is intended to be used primarily as a reference aid and includes data on most of the governments of the world.

FINANCIAL INFORMATION RESOURCES

EDGAR — http://www.sec.gov/edgar.shtml
The Electronic Data Gathering, Analysis, and Retrieval (EDGAR) system is a database from the US Securities and Exchange Commission that contains most of the forms and reports of every publicly traded US company.

Investopedia.com — http://www.investopedia.com
Basic information about the world of publicly traded investments, as well as a source of financial information tools such as a dictionary of financial and investing terms and tutorials on stocks, stock markets, and mutual funds.

Rich Kid Smart Kid — http://richkidsmartkid.com
Created by the Foundation for Financial Literacy, this site is dedicated to increasing the financial literacy of children. There are extensive resources for children, including online financial education games. There are also grade-specific activities that educators can use to understand the basics of finance and entrepreneurship.

Teen Startups — http://www.teenstartups.com
This site, which is part of Entrepreneur.com, has a number of how-to guides for starting a business, and stories of teens and young adults who have created successful businesses.

Teen Business Link — http://www.sba.gov/teens/
Created by the US Small Business Administration, this site offers information on the fundamentals of starting and running a small business.

NEWS AND WEATHER RESOURCES

British Broadcasting Corporation (BBC) — http://news.bbc.co.uk
The online version of one of the British television and radio news organizations has links to news specific to several major regions of the world, as well news in areas such as science, technology, health, and entertainment.

Cable News Network (CNN) — http://www.cnn.com
The online version of the 24-hour television news network has several sections covering news, politics, sports weather, and entertainment.

Google News — http://news.google.com
Searchable and continuously updated resource for news from more than 4,500 news sources. Has sections covering news, business, science, entertainment, health, and sports.

UM Weather — http://cirrus.sprl.umich.edu/wxnet/
This University of Michigan site provides access to thousands of forecasts, images, software, and maps.

Unisys Weather — http://weather.unisys.com
This site has an extensive selection of satellite and graphical weather information. Although intended for meteorologists, there are ample detailed explanations for the novice user.

Vaisala Lightning Explorer — http://thunderstorm.vaisala.com
Visual display of lightning activity across the United States.

Weather Underground — http://www.wunderground.com
This comprehensive weather site has extensive resources for regions outside of North America.

The Weather Channel — http://www.weather.com
Associated with the cable network of the same name, this site features current conditions and forecasts for more than 77,000 locations worldwide.

Yahoo! News and Media Directory — http://dir.yahoo.com/News_and_Media/
This comprehensive media directory contains thousands of links to web sites of newspapers, magazines, television stations, and many other types of media outlets.

HOMEWORK AND STUDY RESOURCES

AOL@School — http://www.aolatschool.com
A directory of educational resources for kindergarten through high school, with sections for students and teachers.

Awesome Library — http://www.awesomelibrary.org
A directory of more than 30,000 educational resources for kindergarten through high school with different sections aimed at children, parents, and teachers.

How-To-Study.com — http://www.how-to-study.com
A study skills resource site with free advice on study skills, study strategies, and study tips in areas such as test taking, reading comprehension, and writing techniques.

Infoplease Homework Center — http://www.infoplease.com/homework/
Drawing on the resources of the Infoplease.com site, this section of that site serves as a directory to resources for the subject areas of writing, geography, history, language arts, mathematics, science, and social studies. It also includes links for research and study skills.

WRITING AND LITERATURE RESOURCES

Bob's Byway — http://www.poeticbyway.com
A poetry resource site that includes a glossary of poetic terms, plus examples of poetic terms from the works of prominent poets, and tips for the enjoyment of poetry.

The Columbia Guide to Online Style — http://www.columbia.edu/cu/cup/cgos2006/basic.html
An online guide for creating formal humanities style and scientific style citations for material taken from online sources such as web sites, blogs, audio files, video files, graphic files, email, databases, and other online content.

The Complete Works of William Shakespeare — http://www-tech.mit.edu/Shakespeare/works.html
This site from the Massachusetts Institute of Technology is one of the earlier Web resources featuring the complete works of Shakespeare.

Dr. Grammar — http://www.drgrammar.org/faqs/
This resource from the University of Northern Iowa answers questions about the proper use of words, punctuation, and grammar.

Encyclopedia Mythica — http://www.pantheon.org
An online encyclopedia of mythology, folklore, and religion that is divided by continent, with further subdivisions to make searching easier. The site also has hundreds of images containing many kinds of deities, heroes, and strange creatures of every description.

Mr. William Shakespeare and the Internet — http://shakespeare.palomar.edu
This resource from Palomar College is a comprehensive annotated guide to the scholarly Shakespeare resources available on Internet.

RhymeZone — http://www.rhymezone.com
A search engine for rhymes where the user enters a word or phrase and the site provides suggested rhyming words, as well as synonyms, definitions, and other information.

The Poetry Archive — http://www.poetryarchive.org
This site contains a collection of recordings of poets reading their own work, with sections of the site for students, teachers, and children.

Punctuation Made Simple — http://lilt.ilstu.edu/golson/punctuation/
This grammar resource from Illinois State University provides visitors with a general idea of how to use colons, semicolons, commas, dashes, and apostrophes.

Purdue University Online Writing Lab — http://owl.english.purdue.edu/owl/
This writing resource site has tutorials on grammar, sentence structure, English for non-native writers of English, creative writing, technical writing, and citation styles.

University of Wisconsin Writing Center — http://www.wisc.edu/writing/Handbook/
A concise resource on basic writing, including the stages of the writing process, advice on grammar and punctuation, and tips on improving writing style.

Vocabulary University — http://www.vocabulary.com
Aimed at students from the fourth grade through high school, this site contains interactive word puzzles that help a student acquire and retain vocabulary. Each session has three levels of difficulty. Each level has three puzzles with 12 words each (36 words in a session) and contains seven additional activities and exercises that help develop vocabulary.

EARTH AND SPACE RESOURCES

Earthquake Hazards Program — http://earthquake.usgs.gov
Continuously updated data on earthquakes in the US that are at least magnitude 2.5 and earthquakes elsewhere in the world that are of magnitude 4.0 and above.

Heavens-Above.com — http://www.heavens-above.com
Provides detailed information about overflights of satellites that are visible to the naked eye, including the International Space Station and Space Shuttle.

University of Alaska Aurora Forecasts — http://www.gedds.alaska.edu/AuroraForecast/

This site of the University of Alaska's Geophysical Institute provides short-term and long-term forecasts for observing the aurora borealis.

MATH AND SCIENCE RESOURCES

Are You Better than Average? — http://www.airsafe.com/analyze/average.htm

Using only a pair of dice, this game demonstrates three basic priciples of applied math: averages, probability, and modeling.

Ask Dr. Math — http://mathforum.org/dr.math/

This part of the Math Forum site at Drexel University is a question-and-answer service for math students and their teachers from kindergarten to high school.

Exploratorium — http://www.exploratorium.edu

This science museum site contains instructions for more than 500 science experiments, podcasts, and interactive exhibits.

Internet Mathematics Library — http://mathforum.org/library/

This site from Drexel University has a catalog of mathematics and mathematics education web sites. Subjects covered include basic math, number theory, algebra, calculus, math history, probability, statistics, operations research, and mathematical applications in engineering, science, and other fields.

Los Alamos National Laboratory Periodic Table of the Elements — http://periodic.lanl.gov

This site, intended as a resource for students from grade school to high school, has historical and scientific information about each element, as well as periodic tables that can be downloaded as PDF or Microsoft Word files. The entire site can also be downloaded as a PDF file.

Math2.org — http://www.math2.org

A collection of tables, graphical models, formulas, and other mathematical information for trigonometry and calculus.

WebElements — http://www.webelements.com

Created by Dr. Mark Winter of the University of Sheffield in the United Kingdom, this site has extensive information on the properties and atomic structure of the elements in periodic table.

Webmath — http://www.webmath.com

This site features many categories of mathematics where a user can find guidance. Once in the general category of interest, a visitor can use a math fill-in-the-blank forms to type in a math problem of interest. The output may be either the answer or guidance to find an answer.

MEDICAL AND HEALTH RESOURCES

MedTerms Medical Dictionary — http://www.medterms.com

This online medical dictionary is the medical reference for MedicineNet.com, containing explanations of more than 16,000 medical terms.

Merck Manual of Medical Information – http://www.merck.com/mmhe/
This searchable site explains disorders, their symptoms, how they are diagnosed, how they might be prevented, and how they can be treated.

Traveler's Health – http://www.cdc.gov/travel/
This site for the US Centers for Disease Control has specific information about world travel health related risks, including specific warnings of disease outbreaks.

EDUCATION AND RESEARCH RESOURCES

MIT OpenCourseWare – http://ocw.mit.edu
This site from the Massachusetts Institute of Technology makes MIT course materials that are used in the teaching of almost all undergraduate and graduate subjects freely available online for any educator, student, or self-motivated learner anywhere in the world.

Nobelprize.org – http://www.nobelprize.org
This official web site of the Nobel Foundation includes information on all prize winners as well as a collection of educational games.

UTOPIA – http://utopia.utexas.edu
This directory provides free public access to the knowledge, research, and information from the libraries, museums, galleries and laboratories of the University of Texas at Austin. There are also sections designed for students and educators from elementary school through high school.

Appendix 2—Online Resources

AUDIO AND VIDEO ENTERTAINMENT

AOL Video — http://video.aol.com
Thousands of videos are available for viewing, and registered users can upload videos. Only a portion of the videos on this site are free. Materials containing illegal, pornographic or harmful material are not allowed. A Family Filter option is also available.

FreshPodcasts.com — http://www.freshpodcasts.com
Links to recent podcasts, podcasting resources, and related software tools.

Internet Movie Database — http://www.imdb.com
This site contains a database of detailed information about more than 350,000 movies and television shows from around the world. Production data provided includes titles, alternative titles, actors, directors, producers, writers, filming location, and country of origin.

MusicUnited.org — http://www.musicunited.org
This coalition of music industry organizations and music artist organizations provides sources where a user can legally buy music online, as well as general guidelines on how to avoid violating the rights of copyright holders.

The Oracle of Bacon — http://www.oracleofbacon.org
Based on information from the Internet Movie Database, this University of Virginia site allows users to play the *Six Degrees of Kevin Bacon* game where the objective is to see how closely linked an actor or actress is to a movie role played by the actor Kevin Bacon.

Google Video — http://video.google.com
Tens of thousands of videos are available for viewing, and registered users can upload their own videos. Sexually explicit material, graphic violence, hateful content, or other material inappropriate for young viewers is not allowed on Google Video. Because of limited pre-screening, such material may be uploaded, but is usually not accessible for long.

Yahoo! Video — http://video.yahoo.com
Using Yahoo! Search, users can view videos that were uploaded to Yahoo!, or will be linked to videos elsewhere on the Web. Although adult materials are not allowed to be uploaded, you can link to adult content from outside of Yahoo! However, you have the option of setting up the video search feature to filter adult material.

YouTube — http://youtube.com
Millions of videos are available for viewing, and users can upload their own video creations as well. Users who upload videos can choose to either let the general public see the videos, or they can restrict access. YouTube.com's policy states that children under the age of 13 are not allowed on the site, and children from 13 to 17 can visit only with their parents' permission. Material meant for adults is available on the site, and can only be accessed only after registering as a user.

PHOTO SHARING RESOURCES

Flickr — http://www.flickr.com
This site allows you to upload photos from the Web, by email, from home computers, or from mobile devices. You must have a Yahoo! account to use the service.

Picasa Web Albums — http://picasaweb.google.com
This site, used in conjunction with the Picasa photo organizer listed in appendix 1, allows you to share photos online.

Appendix 3

Internet Use Agreements

In This Appendix
- Sample Agreement for an Older Child
- Sample Agreement for a Younger Child
- Suggested Ground Rules for Being Online

The following agreements are examples that you may want to use in your own family. They may contain more than what you want to include in a formal agreement, or they may leave out a few areas that you want to include. Feel free to use these sample agreements as well as any other information available on the Speedbrake.com site, to help create your own Internet Use Agreements. These agreements are available in the Family Forms Pack at http://forms.speedbrake.com.

Sample Agreement for an Older Child

General Rules
- I understand which sites I can visit and which ones are off limits.
- I will follow these same rules when I am at home, in school, at the library, or at a friend's home.
- If I come across something that is off limits or that is potentially dangerous, I will tell my parents or another responsible adult.
- I promise to use computers and the Internet to help me and my family pursue the following goals or values:

Privacy
- I will not give out my name, address, telephone number, or any other personal information about my family or myself to anyone online without my parents' permission.
- I will not hide anything about what I do online from my parents. If my parents ask, I will let them look at any file I have on any computer, in any online account, or on any data storage device.
- I will not order or buy anything online without getting my parents' permission.
- I will not post anything online without my parents' permission.
- I will not download any file without getting my parents' permission.

- I will not send a picture or other file to anyone else unless I get my parents' permission.
- I will tell my parents the user name, password, or any other information they need to get into any online account or online service that I have.

Security
- I will not install any software on any computer without getting my parents' permission.
- I will not open any file sent to me unless I get my parents' permission.
- I will allow my parents to access any account or look at any of my data any time they ask.
- I will not keep any secrets from my parents when it comes to what I do online.
- I will not meet or agree to meet in person anyone I have only met online unless I have my parents' permission.
- I will be careful when I use the family's computer equipment.
- I will not let someone else use any of the family's computer equipment, without first getting my parent's permission.

Online Behavior
- I will not use the Internet to bully anyone or to embarrass anyone.

I have read and understood these rules. (Signed by child)

I promise to do my part by being fair and reasonable when it comes to these rules. (Signed by parent).

SAMPLE AGREEMENT FOR A YOUNGER CHILD

- I will not go online alone. If I am online, I must be with a parent or another responsible person.
- If my parents say that I can't do something on the computer, I will obey them.

_____

(Signed by child)

_____

I promise to help my child learn about the Internet. (Signed by parent).

SUGGESTED GROUND RULES FOR BEING ONLINE

As you become more familiar with how you and your child use the computer, you will come up with rules on what your child is allowed to do online. The following suggested rules are ones that would best fit the philosophy of this book. If you have ideas for additional rules, write them down in the spaces provided at the end of the list. These suggested rules are also available in the Family Forms Pack at http://forms.speedbrake.com.

1. Parents make the rules when it comes to using the computer and the Internet.
2. Parents should respect a child's privacy, but any parent has the right to look at any file or get into any account at any time, so parents need to know every password, user name, or screen name of every account or service that a child uses.
3. Parents must approve of any software that will be added to any computer at home.
4. The rules apply at home and away from home.
5. Being online is a privilege, not a right.
6. Everyone should do their best to protect their personal privacy, and the privacy of others.
7. Everyone should do their best to stay safe online.
8. Everyone should help each other learn about computers and the Internet.
9. Don't do anything online that you want to keep a secret or that will embarrass you if made public.
10. If something unexpected or scary happens while you are online or on the computer, tell someone.
11. _____
12. _____

Glossary

Acceptable Use—A set of rules or guidelines that limit how a resource such as Internet access may be used.

Adware—Software that allows advertising to appear while the user is online and possibly when the user is offline. Adware may be included as part of another software program. See also *Malware, Spyware, Trojan Horse, Virus,* and *Worm*.

Antispyware Software—Software designed to detect or remove spyware, or to prevent spyware from being installed. See also *Virus, Antivirus Software, Firewall,* and *Spyware*.

Antivirus Software—Software designed to detect or remove software viruses from a single computer or from a computer network. See also *Antispyware Software, Firewall, Spyware,* and *Virus*.

Application—A computer program that is designed to do a particular task, such as browsing or games.

Attachment—A file that is sent as part of an email message. See also *Bcc, Body, Cc, From, Header, Subject,* and *To*.

Backup—A copy of data, software, or other information that is ideally stored in a place physically separate from the original information.

Bandwidth—A measure of the capacity of a communication channel, such as the rate that data can flow through an Internet connection, typically measured in bits per second. See also *Bit* and *Binary*.

Bcc—*Blind Carbon Copy*. This is one of the three address fields in the header of an email. This field is not visible to the recipient of an email. See also *Email, Header, Subject, From, To, Body, Attachment,* and *Cc*.

Binary—Information made up entirely of ones or zeros.

Bit—*Binary Digit*. A single-digit number that takes on the value of either one or zero.

Blind Carbon Copy—See *Bcc*.

Blog—Short for Web log, this is a journal or diary that is available on the Web. The content could include text, graphics, or other media.

Body—The portion of an email that contains the message. See also *Header*, *Subject*, *From*, *To*, *Cc*, *Attachment*, and *Bcc*.

Bookmark—A web browser feature that allows a user to store the location of a web page or other online resource so that it can be quickly accessed later without typing the full address of the resource.

Broadband—The term is commonly used to refer to Internet access via cable modems, DSL, and wireless technologies where the bandwidth is usually significantly higher than that of a dial-up connection. See also *Bandwidth*, *DSL*, *Dial-up*, *Cable Modem*, and *Wireless Connection*.

Browse—To follow links in a page to get from one resource to another on the Web.

Browser—A software program such as Internet Explorer or Firefox that allows a computer to interpret, display, or access information from the Internet. The information displayed is typically some combination of text, graphics, and sound. See also *Client*.

Buddy List—A feature of the AOL Instant Messenger instant messaging program that allows a user to view the online status and sometimes the profile of selected users. See also *Contact List*, *Profile*, *Social Networking*, and *IM*.

Bulletin Board—See *Newsgroup*.

Burn—To write data to a compact disc. This term is usually used in the context of copying a music file or some other kind of audio file onto a compact disc. See also *Rip*.

Byte—A unit of measure of computer memory that is equal to eight binary digits or roughly one character of information. See also *Kilobyte*, *Megabyte*, and *Gigabyte*.

Cable Modem — A connection to the Internet using a cable connection that is separate from a telephone line. The cable may be dedicated for Internet access or it may carry other data such as television signals. See also *Dial-up, Wireless Connection,* and *DSL.*

Carbon Copy — See *Cc.*

Cc — *Carbon Copy.* This is one of the three address fields in the header of an email. Any recipient will be able to see any address listed in this field. See also *Email, Header, Subject, From, To, Body, Attachment,* and *Bcc.*

CD-ROM — *Compact Disc Read-Only Memory.* A computer storage medium for digitized information, including data and computer programs. See also *DVD.*

Chain Letter — An email that encourages the recipient to forward the message to several others. See also *Spam* and *Forward.*

Chat — Any form of interactive online communication that takes place in real time, typically through either a web site or through instant messaging software. Communication can be by text, audio, or video.

Chat Room — An online resource that allows two or more users to type messages that can be viewed almost instantly by other active users. The conversation is usually text based, and ongoing conversations are accessible to everyone in the chat room, even those who are not typing messages. See also *IM, Lurker, Screen Name,* and *Real Time.*

Check Box — A small square target area that a user can select in order to choose from a list of options, typically on a form or dialog box. Once selected, a check mark is placed within the square. See also *Radio Button.*

Child Pornography — Any kind of visual depiction that shows a person under the age of 18 engaged in sexually explicit conduct. The conduct does not have to involve either sexual acts or nudity. In the United States, it is illegal to produce, transmit, buy, sell, trade, or possess such material. See also *Pornography* and *Obscene.*

Child Predator—Any adult who actively works to develop a personal relationship with a child in order to cause some future harm either from an inappropriate or illegal online or offline relationship. See also *Pedophile*.

Client—A program on a computer or other device that requests services of information from a server. Servers are typically used to store or generate information that is requested by a client program. See also *Server*.

Contact List—The group of people who are allowed to have an online relationship with a user, and who can view that user's online status and online profile. See also *Buddy List*, *Social Networking*, *IM*, and *Chat Room*.

Content—The text, graphics, and other information that is contained in an email, web page, or file.

Cookies—A small text file that a web site's server places on a computer that allows a browser to retain specific information about a web site visit. Such information may include things like a user name, user preferences, or pages visited. When the user makes a return visit, the web site's server collects and uses information stored in that file. See also *Third-Party Cookies*.

Copyright—A form of intellectual property protection that is provided by the laws of most countries. In general, it applies to most written and visual works. It is usually necessary to get the permission of a copyright holder before using a copyrighted work. See also *Fair Use*, *Intellectual Property*, and *Piracy*.

CPU—*Central Processing Unit*. This is the integrated circuit chip that performs the data processing and interprets the instructions given by the software and by the user. For a desktop computer, this term also refers to the component containing all the basic hardware, including the hard drive.

Crash—An unexpected shutdown of either a software program or a computer. Often, the system or program may remain active, but ceases to respond to a user's input.

Creative Commons License — A form of intellectual property license that allows works to be created and used under that license that is somewhere between full copyright protection and public domain. See also *Public Domain* and *Copyright*.

Cyberbullying — Repeated or coordinated cruel or harassing actions directed at an individual by means of email, instant message, text message, blogs, web sites, or other Internet-related means.

Cyberspace — The nonphysical reality created by a computer or by a network of computers. The term is often used as a metaphor for describing the Internet.

Data — A collection of unorganized facts that have not yet been processed into useful information.

Database — A collection of related information, stored in either physical or electronic form, which is focused on a particular subject or discipline.

Decryption — Decoding or unscrambling data in a way that will recreate the original data prior to being encrypted by the sender. See also *Secure Socket Layer* and *Encryption*.

Defamation — A false statement that causes harm to someone's reputation, or that causes that person to become a target of public contempt, hatred, ridicule, or condemnation. If the statement is spoken, it is referred to as slander, and if written or broadcast, as libel. See also *Libel* and *Slander*.

Default — The initial or basic settings of a software program or hardware device.

Defragment — The automated process of rearranging files and programs on a hard drive in order to allow a computer to run more efficiently.

Delete — To remove or erase.

Desktop — A personal computer that is composed of several components including a keyboard, display device, and a separate unit that contains the data, software, and the electronics. This also refers to the icons and other graphics visible on a computer's display when no applications are running. See also *Laptop*.

258 Parenting and the Internet

Dialog Box — A small window that appears within a larger display that either presents information or requests input. See also *Toolbar, Menu Bar,* and *Pull-down Menu*.

Dial-up — An Internet connection that requires the exclusive use of a standard phone line. See also *DSL, Cable Modem,* and *Wireless Connection*.

Digital — Relating to information that is transmitted or stored as a series of binary digits.

Digital Subscriber Line — See *DSL*.

Directory — Online, a directory is a service that organizes links to Internet resources by category or by some other criteria. In a personal computer, a directory is an index of the contents of the files in a part of the hard drive, containing information such as the name of a file, the size of a file, and the file's creation date. See also *Folder*.

Display — A screen or similar device that is used in conjunction with a personal computer.

Domain Name — This is the unique combination of numbers and characters that helps to identify the location of web pages or other Web resources. For example, in the URL http://www.airsafe.com, the domain name is airsafe.com. See also *URL*.

Download — The transfer of data or files from one computer to another. See also *Download* and *Server*.

Drop-down Menu — See *Pull-down Menu*.

DSL — *Digital Subscriber Line*. A technology for high-speed Internet access using standard phone lines that allows the line to be simultaneously used for Internet access and for making and receiving phone calls. DSL bandwidth is typically higher than the bandwidth of a dial-up connection and lower than that of a cable modem. See also *Dial-up, Cable Modem,* and *Broadband*.

DVD — *Digital Video Disc*. A computer storage medium for digitized information, including computer programs and data. It is similar to a CD-ROM, but stores much more data. See also *CD-ROM*.

Email — *Electronic Mail*. A generic term for messages composed and transmitted on a computer network. See also *Header*, *Subject*, *From*, *To*, *Cc*, and *Bcc*.

E-mail — See *Email*.

Encryption — The coding or scrambling of information in a way that can only be decoded or unscrambled by the recipient. See also *Secure Socket Layer* and *Decryption*.

End User License Agreement — See *EULA*.

ESSID — *Extended Service Set Identifier*. See also *SSID*.

EULA — A software creator's or online service provider's legal terms for using a product or service. See also *Privacy Policy*.

Executable File — A file that once opened or selected begins to run a software program.

Extension — The group of letters in a file name that occur after the period and that identify the type of file. For example, in the file name "example.txt," the extension "txt" indicates that the file is a plain text file.

External hard drive — This is a hard drive that is not built into a laptop or desktop computer, but that can be connected to a computer. Typically this kind of drive has much greater capacity than other portable data storage devices. See also *Hard Drive*.

FAQ — *Frequently Asked Questions*. A list of commonly asked questions about a subject.

Fair Use — The legal use of copyrighted material without the permission of the copyright holder. See also *Copyright* and *Piracy*.

Favorites — See *Bookmark*.

File — An organized collection of data that can be saved or retrieved by a computer. Typical file types include, audio files, graphics files, text files, and video files.

File Extension — See *Extension*.

File Name—The name of a computer file. Usually, such names include a file name extension that is specific to the format of the file. For example, "partylist.mp3" is an audio file, and "partylist.txt" is a plain text file.

File Sharing—Accessing files on one computer from a different computer while using the Internet as the conduit for the data. See also *Peer-to-Peer Networking*.

Filter—Software or settings that limit the content that can be displayed or accessed by a computer.

Firefox—A browser developed by the Mozilla Foundation. This is open source software that is available as a free download. See also *Internet Explorer, Open Source, Download,* and *Browser*.

Firewall—Software that prevents unauthorized access to a computer connected to the Internet. See also *Antivirus Software*.

First Amendment—An amendment to the Constitution of the United States that among other things guarantees freedom of speech and freedom of the press. See also *Free Speech*.

Flash Drive—A portable device that is used to store data. Also known as a thumb drive, USB drive, or memory stick. Unlike a hard drive, this device does not contain any moving parts. See also *Hard Drive*.

Folder—An index of the contents of the files in a part of the hard drive, containing information such as the name of a file, the size of a file, and the file's creation date. See also *Directory*.

Forward—To redirect or resend an incoming email to one or more recipients. Many email applications will add an abbreviation like "Fw:" or "Fwd:" to the beginning of the subject line to indicate that the email originated with someone other than the previous sender.

Free Software—Software that can be obtained and used without cost, can be used for any purpose, and that can also be copied and distributed without cost. See also *Open Source*.

Glossary 261

Free Speech—The right to express opinions, information, or ideas in public or in private, regardless of content, without interference by a government. See also *First Amendment*.

Freeware—See *Free Software*.

Frequently Asked Questions—See *FAQ*.

From—The field in the header of an email that identifies the sender of an email message. See also *To, From, Cc, Body, Attachment,* and *Bcc*.

GIF—*Graphics Interchange Format*. This is one of the common formats for encoding photographs and other visual information. GIF encoded files have the ".gif" extension.

Gigabyte—A unit of measure, equivalent to 1024 megabytes, that is used to compare data storage capacity. See also *Byte, Kilobyte,* and *Megabyte*.

Graphics—Generic term for the visual content in a document or web page.

Graphics Interchange Format—See *GIF*.

Grooming—A process used by child predators to gain the trust of a potential victim of child sexual abuse by first building an online relationship using communications tools such as email, chat rooms, and instant messaging. See also *IM, Chat Room,* and *Child Predator*.

Hacker—Someone who attempts to gain unauthorized access to a computer or computer network.

Harassment—Words or actions that contribute to a hostile social environment and are directed at an individual or group based on characteristics such as gender, race, or age.

Hard Drive—A high-capacity data storage medium that contains the data and programs that are used by a computer. This device can be located within a computer or separate from the computer. See also *External Hard Drive*.

Header—The portion of an email that identifies the sender and recipients of the message, and sometimes other information such as the date and time the message was sent. See also *Email, Subject, From, To, Body, Attachment,* and *Bcc*.

History — A record of the web pages or other online resources that have been visited.

Home Page — The page on a web site that serves as the central focus or starting point for site visitors. Often, the address of the home page is the domain name preceded by "www."

Host — A computer that is connected directly to the Internet rather than indirectly, such as through the computers of an ISP.

Hot Spot — A location that has wireless Internet connections available to the public.

HTML — *HyperText Markup Language.* A computer language that is used to control how a browser displays a web page and how a web page is linked to other Web resources.

HTTP — *HyperText Transfer Protocol.* A protocol or set of rules used by servers and browsers for sending information across the Web. The characters "http://" that appear at the beginning of a URL refer to this protocol. See also *Server* and *Browser*.

Hyperlink — See *Link*.

Hypertext — Any document that contains one or more links to other documents. The links may be embedded within a word or phrase in the text, or within some other element such as a picture.

Hypertext Link — See *Link*.

HyperText Markup Language — See *HTML*.

HyperText Transfer Protocol — See *HTTP*.

Icon — A graphical representation of an item that when selected causes some kind of reaction or response such as starting a program or opening a file.

Identity Theft — The unauthorized use of personal information such as name, Social Security number, or date of birth in order to take on the identity of another person, often for the purpose of committing a crime.

IM—*Instant Messaging* or *Instant Message*. An online service that allows near instant text-based communication among two or more individuals. Can also refer to the content of a message sent using this technology. See also *Chat Room*.

Inbox—The default destination for incoming email in most email programs.

Information—Any communication or reception of knowledge such as facts, data, or opinions that can be transmitted, accessed, or stored using some medium.

Information Superhighway—See *Cyberspace*.

Instant Message or Instant Messaging—See *IM*.

Intellectual Property—Products of human intellectual effort such as inventions, musical performances, or written works that may be protected or controlled through copyrights, trademarks, or through other means. See also *Copyright*, *Fair Use*, and *Piracy*.

Internet—A worldwide collection of computer networks that uses several protocols whereby computers and other devices can communicate with each other. Email, instant messaging, and the Web are three of the most widely used applications on the Internet. See also *Cyberspace*.

Internet Explorer—A browser designed to work with the Windows operating system. See also *Firefox, Windows, Open Source, Download,* and *Browser*.

Internet Service Provider—See *ISP*.

Intranet—A computer network inside an organization that uses the same kinds of software and communications protocols as the publicly accessible Internet, but which is not accessible by users outside of the organization. See also *Internet*.

IP—*Internet Protocol*. The standard protocol used by computer networks and other systems or devices to communicate within the Internet.

IP Address—The numeric address of a computer, server, or other device that is connected to the Internet.

ISP—*Internet Service Provider.* An entity, usually a commercial enterprise, which provides access to the Internet, typically for a monthly fee.

JPEG—*Joint Pictures Expert Group.* This is a common format for encoding photographs and other graphics. JPEG encoded files have the ".jpg" extension.

Junk Email—See *Spam.*

Key Phrase—Several words, usually enclosed with quotation marks, that are used in a search engine to locate online resources. See *Keyword* and *Search Engine.*

Key Site—A web site that provides a level of information or a level of service that is better than most or all of the available alternatives.

Keyword—A word that is used within a search engine to locate resources online. Search engines can process one or more of these words at a time. See *Key Phrase* and *Search Engine.*

Kilobyte—A unit of measure, equal to 1024 bytes, used to compare data storage capacity. See also *Byte* and *Megabyte.*

Laptop—A portable personal computer that contains within a single package a keyboard, data storage medium, display screen, and all the other necessary components. See also *Desktop.*

Libel—A false statement, written or broadcast, and that causes harm to someone's reputation, or that causes that person to become a target of public contempt, hatred, ridicule, or condemnation. See also *Defamation* and *Slander.*

Link—These are coded parts of a web page that when selected allow a browser to access some other resource on the Internet. A link may appear as highlighted, colored, or underlined text, or as part of another element of a web page, such as a picture or some other graphical element.

Log Off—To disconnect from the Internet, from some other computer network, from a computer, or from some kind of application or online service.

Log On — To use a combination of a user name and a password to connect to the Internet, to a computer, to an application, or to an online service. See also *User Name* and *Password*.

Lurker — A person who may visit a chat room to read what other people type, but who remains anonymous by not posting any messages.

Mailing List — A list of email addresses that is managed by an organization or an individual and that is used to send email to those on the list.

Malicious Software — Any software designed to cause harm to a computer or the person using that computer. Effects may include slowing computer performance, tracking browsing habits, or stealing passwords or other valuable information. See also *Virus, Worm, Adware, Trojan Horse,* and *Spyware*.

Malware — See *Malicious Software*.

Media Player — Software that is able to play one or more types of audio and video files.

Megabyte — A unit of measure, equal to 1024 kilobytes, used to compare data storage capacity. See also *Byte, Kilobyte,* and *Gigabyte*.

Menu — A list of items, options, or commands that can be selected by the user. See also *Menu Bar, Pull-down Menu,* and *Toolbar*.

Menu Bar — A row of menu titles, usually at or near the top of a window, that when selected commands the program to perform some action or function. See also *Pull-down Menu, Menu,* and *Toolbar*.

Minor — A child under the age of 18.

Modem — A device that allows a computer to communicate with other devices or with the Internet.

Monitor — See *Display*.

Monitoring Software — Personal computer programs that allow a parent or caregiver to monitor a child's online activity without blocking access. See also *Filter*.

Mouse—This is a device that allows a user to position the cursor or to select icons or objects on the display.

MP3—*Moving Pictures Group Experts Layer 3*. This is a format for a type of audio file that is often used for music and podcasts. This kind of file has an ".mp3" file extension.

Multimedia—A file, web page, or other resource that contains more than one type of information, usually a combination of audio, graphic, or text information.

Net—See *Internet*.

Network—A group of two or more computers that are able to communicate with one another.

Newsgroup—An online community that is dedicated to the discussion of a particular topic. The discussion usually consists of posts on a topic and responses to those posts. See also *Post*.

Notebook—See *Laptop*.

Obscene—Material that a judge or jury has determined to be sexually explicit, offensive to conventional standards of decency, and lacking in serious literary, scientific, political, or artistic, value. See also *Pornography*.

Office Application Suite—A group of programs used to create documents and perform functions appropriate for a business or academic environment. This group of programs typically includes a spreadsheet, word processor, and presentation manager. It may also include a database management program. See also *Spreadsheet, Database, Presentation Manager,* and *Word Processor*.

Offline—Used to describe information, resources, or activities that are not associated with accessing a computer network. Also used to describe the state of a system that has the capability to be online but that is not currently online.

Online—Used to describe the activities that involve accessing a computer network such as the Internet.

Online Profiling — The practice of compiling information about a user by tracking actions such as sites visited and items purchased. Personal information volunteered by the user or supplied by a third party may also be included.

Open Source — Software or other intellectual property that is freely distributed and can be modified without restriction by users. See also *Intellectual Property*.

Operating System — The basic software of a computer that controls all other software in the computer and any devices that are connected to the computer.

Opt-in — A policy where a user explicitly agrees to allow a web site or some other service provider to collect, use, or share personal information.

Opt out — A policy where a user can explicitly request that a web site or some other provider of a service not collect, use, or share personal information.

Outbox — The temporary file that most email programs use for temporary storage of outgoing email before that email is sent to its intended destination.

Outlook Express — An email program that is included with the Internet Explorer browser of the Microsoft Corporation. See also *Browser*, *Client*, *Email*, and *Internet Explorer*.

Overblocking — A condition where an Internet filter denies access to content that a user is intended to be able to access. See also *Underblocking* and *Filter*.

P2P — See *Peer-to-Peer Networking*.

Parental Controls — Software settings that prevent children from accessing inappropriate Internet content.

Password — A combination of uppercase letters, lowercase letters, numbers, or other characters used to access a program, a computer, or a computer network.

PDF — *Portable Document Format*. This is a document format that can be viewed using a widely available and free PDF document reader. Documents created in a variety of other formats can be saved in this format.

Pedophile — An adult (male or female) who is either sexually attracted to a child or to children, or who engages in sexual activity with a child or with children. See also *Child Predator*.

Peer-to-Peer Network — A type of network where computers exchange files or communicate directly with each other, rather than through a central server. Often referred to as peer-to-peer, or P2P. See also *File Sharing*.

Personal Information — Data that can be used to identify or locate a person. Data includes, but is not limited to, user names, passwords, address, telephone number, job title, school, date of birth, and credit card numbers.

Pharming — A technique used by identity thieves where traffic is redirected from a legitimate web site address to another address, where the potential victim is then encouraged to voluntarily provide personal or financial information. See also *Phishing* and *Privacy*.

Phishing — A technique used by identity thieves or other criminals who use an emails, instant messages, popups, or other online communications to misrepresent their identity in order to obtain the personal or financial information of others. See also *Pharming* and *Privacy*.

Photo Organizer — A type of software that is used to manage the graphics files on a computer.

Photo Sharing — The process of uploading, organizing, and distributing photos or other graphic information online, usually through web sites dedicated to this function.

Piracy — Illegal or unauthorized copying, use, installation, or distribution of intellectual property such as software or music files. See also *Fair Use*, *Copyright*, and *Intellectual Property*.

Plug-in — A small software program that adds features or functions to a larger program.

Podcast — An audio or video file distributed using the Internet. This term also refers to the method of delivery.

Popunder — Also written as pop-under. A type of browser window that behaves like a popup, except that it appears beneath the current browser window rather than on top of the current window. See also *Popup*.

Popup — Also written as pop-up. A type of browser window that appears on top of the current browser window while a user is visiting a web page. See also *Popunder*.

Pornography — Any material that is sexually explicit and that is intended to cause sexual arousal. Such material does not have to involve descriptions or depictions of nudity or sexual activity. In the United States, most forms of sexually explicit material are protected by the First Amendment, making it legal for adults to create, publish, or consume such material. See *Child Pornography, First Amendment,* and *Obscene*.

Post — A message entered into a newsgroup, chat room, web site, or other online resource.

Presentation Manager — A type of software used to create, edit, and display presentations by using a combination of text, drawings, graphics, audio and other media. See also *Office Application Suite*.

Privacy — The ability to control the amount of access that others have to your personal information and the amount of control that others have over your online experience.

Privacy Policy — A written policy associated with a web site that explains how data from users may be collected and used. Such policies may allow the user to opt-in or opt out from activities of the site. See also *EULA*.

Profile — Personal information that a user provides to an online service. Depending on the online service, this information may be accessible to other users of that service and may consist of items such as name, screen name, address, personal interests, photos, or other personal details. See also *Buddy List, IM,* and *Social Networking*.

Program — See *Software* and *Application*.

Public Domain — Intellectual property that is no longer under copyright protection, has failed to meet the requirements for copyright protection, or that was intentionally provided to the public free of copyright restrictions. Works in the public domain may be used freely without the permission of the work's creator or former copyright owner.

Pull-down Menu — A list of options that appears when you select an item on a toolbar. See also *Toolbar* and *Dialog Box*.

Radio Button — A small circular target area that a user can select in order to choose from a list of options, typically on a form or dialog box. Once selected, the interior of the circle usually changes to a dark color. See also *Check Box*.

Real Time — Interaction between two or more users or systems that occurs without any apparent delays.

Reformat — The process of erasing all files and programs on a hard drive, and reinstalling the operating system. See also *Hard Drive* and *Operating System*.

Registered User — A person who has to go through some kind of registration process in order to use a particular online service. See also *User*.

Rip — To copy data from a compact disc to either a personal computer hard drive or to some other storage media. This term is usually used in the context of copying a music file or other audio file from a compact disc. See also *Burn*.

Router — A device that connects two or more networks. See also *Modem, Wi-Fi, Wireless Connection,* and *Wireless Network*.

Save — A command used to update a file with any editing changes. In most programs, this overwrites the previous version of the file.

Scam — A fraudulent scheme that usually involves one or more voluntary actions on the part of the victim.

Screen Name — An alias or pseudonym someone uses while communicating online. See also *Chat Room, IM,* and *User Name*.

Search — The act of looking for online resources through the use of a search engine or directory. See also *Search Engine* and *Directory*.

Search Box — An input field for search engine commands.

Search Engine — An online service that allows a user to find online resources by using one or more keywords or key phrases. Most search engines present the results of a search as a list of web pages where the position on that list depends on how well that page's contents match the search terms. See also *Directory*.

Secure Socket Layer — An Internet industry standard for encrypting and protecting information that is transmitted over the Internet. The URL for this kind of protocol begins with "https://" rather than the "http://" that is normally used.

Security — The ability to identify, manage, or eliminate threats to information, to technology, or to the well-being of a group or an individual.

Select — To choose an option in a program or web page by using either a mouse or keyboard commands.

Server — A computer that responds to requests for services or for information made by other computers in a network.

Service Mark — A combination of one or more words, symbols, or designs that distinguish services provided by one party from those provided by others. See also *Copyright*, *Trademark*, and *Intellectual Property*.

Service Set Identifier — See *SSID*.

Signature Block — The block of text at the end of the body of an email that typically has the sender's name and contact information. See also *Signature File* and *Email*.

Signature File — A short text file containing the signature block information that is placed at the end of an email message. See also *Signature Block* and *Email*.

Site — See *Web Site*.

Slander—A false statement that is spoken and that causes harm to someone's reputation, or that causes that person to become a target of public contempt, hatred, ridicule, or condemnation. See also *Defamation* and *Libel*.

Social Engineering—The practice of getting access to sensitive personal information by persuading a potential victim to willingly provide the information or the means to access to the information. See also *Identity Theft*, *Phishing*, and *Spam*.

Social Networking—Online services that encourage personal or group interaction by allowing users to easily publish and exchange information about themselves using online tools and applications such as email, instant messaging, chat rooms and blogs.

Software—A set of logical instructions that either controls the behavior of computers and other electronic devices, or that provides some specific kind of functionality.

Spam—Popular term for unsolicited commercial email, often associated with the promotion of a product or service of questionable value. The term may also be applied to email containing chain letters, fraudulent promotions, and other information that lacks authority, usefulness, or validity.

Spreadsheet—A file type formatted so that an appropriate application will display the data in one or more rectangular grids, and that allows the user to perform calculations on data within the grids. This term also refers to software designed to create, edit, save, and print files of this type. See also *Office Application Suite*.

Spyware—A general term for software that collects data about a user's online activities and sends the information to someone else without the user's permission or knowledge. See also *Adware*, *Virus*, *Worm*, *Trojan Horse*, and *Malware*.

SSID—*Service Set Identifier*. The name that identifies a wireless network. See also *Wireless Network*, *Wireless Connection*, *Router*, *Wi-Fi*, and *Encryption*.

SSL—See *Secure Socket Layer*.

Subject — The field in the header of an email that contains a short description of the email's contents. See also *To, From, Cc, Body,* and *Bcc.*

Surf — To search for information on the Internet without either a goal or a systematic process.

Surge Suppressor — Electrical accessory designed to protect sensitive electronic devices from sudden and significant changes in voltage.

Tab — A visual element, shaped like the tab on a paper file folder, that is used to navigate in a browser window, dialog box, or other part of a display.

Text Editor — A simple word processing program that allows a user to create, edit, and print files containing only text characters, and that usually has very limited formatting options. See also *Word Processor.*

Text Message — A brief electronic message sent and received through a wireless network to or from a wireless device such as a cell phone or pager.

To — The field in the header of an email that identifies the recipients of an email. See also *Subject, From, Cc, Body, Attachment,* and *Bcc.*

Third-Party Cookies — Cookies that are generated from a web site other than the one that the user is visiting.

Thumb Drive — See *Flash Drive.*

Toolbar — A row of words or icons displayed by an active software application that when selected activates a function or performs some kind of action.

Trademark — A combination of one or more words, phrases, symbols, or designs that identifies and distinguishes the source of the goods of one party from those of others. See also *Service Mark, Copyright,* and *Intellectual Property.*

Trojan Horse—A program that is designed to do something malicious to a computer or to a computer network, but that is disguised as a program designed to do something beneficial. See also *Adware, Virus, Worm, Spyware,* and *Malicious Software.*

Underblocking—A condition where an Internet filter permits access to content that a user is not intended to access. See also *Overblocking* and *Filter.*

Uninstall—To remove a program from a computer.

Upload—The transfer of data or of one or more files from a user's computer to a server or to some other computer. See also *Download* and *Server.*

URL—*Uniform Resource Locator.* This is an addressing system that uses a combination of characters and numbers to uniquely identify and locate each resource on the Web. For most web pages, the characters "http://" precede the address. Some browsers do not require a user to type the characters "http://" to recognize the address.

USB—*Universal Serial Bus.* This is common type of computer connection that allows different kinds of hardware to be connected to and communicate with a computer.

User—A person who is accessing an information system or network, either directly or indirectly. See also *Registered User.*

Username—See *User Name.*

User Name—The name used to access a particular application, software program, online application, or network.

User Profile—See *Profile.*

Virus—A computer program designed to make copies of itself without any kind of user action or intervention. This kind of program can spread only after attaching itself to other programs or files, and is often designed to do something malicious to any computer that it infects. See also *Adware, Antivirus Software, Worm,* and *Trojan Horse.*

Voice Over Internet Protocol — Also known as *VOIP* or *VoIP*, this is a protocol and associated technology that allows users to make and receive telephone calls by using an Internet connection.

VOIP — See *Voice Over Internet Protocol.*

Web — A portion of the Internet that allows users to access data and services using a browser.

Web Browser — See *Browser.*

Webcam — A camera that is connected to a computer and that can be used to send live images to a web site, chat room, or some other part of the Internet.

Web Log — See *Blog.*

Web Page — One page of a document on the Web. It is usually a file that is written in HTML and stored on a server. Typically, each page has links to other online resources. Each page on the Web has an address called a Uniform Resource Locator or URL. See also *HTML* and *Server.*

Web Site — A set of related web pages that share a common domain name. See also *Domain Name.*

WEP — *Wired Equivalent Privacy.* An encryption protocol used in wireless networking. See also *Router, Wireless Networking, WPA,* and *Encryption.*

Wi-Fi — *Wireless Fidelity.* A communication protocol that allows computers and other devices to exchange data without the use of wires or cables. See also *Wireless Connection* and *Router.*

Wiki — A web site that allows users to add, remove, or edit content.

Window — A rectangular space on a computer screen that is created by a browser or other software.

Windows — A class of operating system software created by the Microsoft Corporation. The majority of existing personal computers use some variation of Windows.

Windows Explorer — The file management program included with many versions of the Windows operating system.

Wireless Access Point—See *Router*.

Wireless Connection—A method for connecting one or more computers to a network or to the Internet without using cables or wiring. See also *Wi-Fi* and *Router*.

Wireless Network—One or more computers that can access the Internet or that can communicate with one another without being connected by wires or cables. See also *Wi-Fi*, *Wireless Connection*, *Router*, and *Modem*.

Word Processor—Software that allows a user to create, edit, format, display, save, and print documents containing both text and graphics. See also *Office Application Suite*

World Wide Web—See *Web*

Worm—A virus program that can spread to other computers without attaching itself to other programs and without further action from a user. See also *Malicious Software*.

WPA—*Wi-Fi Protected Access*. An encryption protocol used in wireless networking. See also *Router*, *Wireless Networking*, *WEP*, and *Encryption*.

Write—To create or edit, and then save data to some kind of storage medium, such as the hard drive of a personal computer.

WWW—See *Web*.

INDEX

advertising, 44–45, 50, 161, 253
adware, 45, 212, 253
AirSafe.com, 145, 150, 204
American Library Association, 182–83
Are You Better than Average?, 242
attachment, 121, 127, 253
   email etiquette, 125
   email filters, 136
   unwanted email, 130, 131, 136, 138
   viruses, 61–62
   when to use, 121
   See also Gettysburg Criterion
audio resources, 216–17, 245

blog, 16, 104, 195–97, 227, 254
book and library resources, 230–32
bookmark, 165, 254
browser
   advertising, 45
   cookies, 172, 175
   definition, 33, 254
   history file, 165, 170–72, 262
   popular, 16–17, 213
   popups, 44, 45, 50, 52, 53–54, 55–56, 71, 74
   setup, 50–56
   software, 213
   updating, 58, 61
   See also bookmark; cookies; Firefox; Internet Explorer
bullying. *See* cyberbullying

cable modem, 36, 255
chain letter, 120, 130, 131, 132, 255
chat room
   advice for parents, 116, 124, 192–94
   child predators, 109
   cyberbullying, 107
   definition, 255
   desktop search, 218
   issues, 193–94
   lurkers, 193
   risks, 78, 112, 192–94, 223
   screen name, 65
   software, 214

children
   role of, 24–25, 47–48, 105, 185–86
   Internet use agreement, 25, 48–49, 82, 107, 168, 247–51
   free speech, 98, 99, 181
Child Internet Protection Act, 183–84
child pornography
   CyberTipLine, 220
   definition, 96–97, 255
   law enforcement, 113–15
   and pornography, 96–98
   unwanted email, 139
child predator,
   child behavior, 110–11
   contacting victims, 76, 77, 109–11
   definition, 108, 256
   explicit conversation, 110
   grooming, 109–10, 111–13
   IM, 192
   law enforcement, 113–15, 116
   online relationship, 110–11
   personal information, 77, 109, 113
   pornography, 110, 113–14
   prevention, 111–13
   sexual solicitation, 114
   warning signs, 110–11
Clock Is Running, The, 162
computer
   as a tool, 26
   common types, 30
   costs, 37–39
   disposal, 83–84
   hardware, 30–32, 39–40
   ISP, 35
   online resources, 228–29
   and parenting, 21
   placement in home, 39
   software, 32–35, 213–18
   suggested options, 39–40
   wireless connection, 36
   written agreements, 13, 247–51
cookies
   definition, 44, 256
   deleting, 51, 53, 55
   managing, 50–53, 54–55
   reviewing, 172–74

copyright
    books, 91
    definition, 90, 256
    email, 128
    fair use, 92–95, 259
    issues online, 90, 92–95
    music, 91, 94
    not protected by, 91–92
    protected by, 90–91, 92–95
    resources, 225–26
    Shakespeare, 94
    See also piracy; public domain
cyberbullying
    definition, 104, 257
    email, 104, 105, 106, 107–8, 130, 139
    examples, 104–5
    IM, 192
    Internet use agreement, 107
    prevention, 107–8
    responding to, 106
    roles, 105
    warning signs, 105

data storage devices
    backup files, 85
    file transfer, 180
    inappropriate content, 110, 165, 169
    Internet use agreement, 248
    managing, 169, 175, 206
    privacy, 44, 73
    security, 77, 79–80, 87
    tracking process, 85–86
    See also flash drive
defamation, 99–100, 196, 257
desktop computer. *See* computer
desktop search, 40, 175, 218
dial-up connection, 35, 258
dictionary and thesaurus resources, 229–30
directory
    compared to search engine, 147, 151–52
    defined, 147, 258
    limitations, 152
    online resources, 223–25
display, 30–31, 38, 111, 258

educational resources
    books and libraries, 230–32
    dictionary and thesaurus, 229–30
    earth and space, 241–42
    homework help, 182, 238–39
    math and science, 242–43
    news, 237–38
    reference resources, 232–33
    search engines and directories, 223–25
    using a librarian, 185–86
    world geography and politics, 234–36
    writing and literature, 239–41
email
    access, 123
    accounts, 123, 124, 135, 226–27
    addressing, 118–19
    as private information, 42–43
    blind carbon copy, 118–19, 125
    body, 120–21
    child predators, 109
    copyright, 128
    cyberbullying, 104, 106, 107–8
    defamation, 100
    definition, 259
    etiquette, 125
    filtering, 61–63, 136–37
    fraudulent requests, 70–72
    Gettysburg Criterion, 126–27
    grammar and vocabulary, 124
    HTML, 62, 120
    issues, 128
    mailing lists, 64
    malicious software, 61–62
    multiple accounts, 123–24
    online accounts, 124, 226–27
    organizing, 121–22
    parts of, 118–21
    phishing, 44
    pornography, 97, 99
    requests by, 70–72
    Seven Steps to Controlling Email, 132–41
    signature files, 60
    software, 33, 217
    subject line, 119–20
    unsolicited, 42, 120
    See also attachment; Outlook Express; unwanted email

Index 279

encryption, 57, 71–72, 259
ESSID, 56, 259

fair use, 92–95, 259.
  See also copyright
Family Forms Pack
  ground rules, 206–7, 251
  Internet use agreement, 18, 247–50
  managing data, 86, 169, 206
  managing passwords, 68, 72–73
  notebook, 205–6
  tracking online activity, 66, 72–73, 168–69, 206
FBI, 112, 113, 114, 115
file management. *See* Windows Explorer
file sharing, 79, 101, 116, 199–200, 260
filter
  additional software, 137, 169
  definition 260
  email, 60–62, 134–37
  libraries, 183–84, 186, 187
  limitations, 166–67
  online services, 169
  photo sharing, 199
  search engine, 152, 224–25
  spam, 135
  uses of, 166, 175
  viruses, 61–62
  See also inappropriate content
financial education, 236–37
Firefox
  settings, 50–52, 171, 172–73
  and Internet Explorer, 40, 144
  See also browser
firewall, 33, 59, 74, 215, 260
First Amendment, 95–96, 183, 260
flash drive
  data backup, 40, 81, 85
  definition, 31, 260
  file transfer, 40, 180
  inappropriate content, 165
  privacy, 44,
  security, 79–80
  See also data storage devices
fraudulent schemes
  characteristics, 70–71
  common types, 43–44, 130, 132
  filtering email, 135–37
  information requests, 70–72, 78

fraudulent schemes (*continued*)
  security, 76, 78, 79
  See also phishing; scam
free speech
  at school, 181
  children, 98, 99
  definition 261
  email, 99, 128
  library, 188
  organizations, 225
  pornography and, 95–96
  See also defamation; First Amendment

geography resources, 218, 234–36
Gettysburg Criterion, 126–27
Gmail, 118, 227. *See also* email
Google
  book search, 231
  desktop search, 40, 175, 218
  email, 118, 227
  evaluating inbound links, 160
  filtering, 224
  geography reference, 218
  maps, 234
  modeling software, 218
  news, 237
  photo organizer, 216
  photo sharing, 246
  video, 246
  web site, 224
  See also search
grooming, 109–10, 112–13, 261.
  See also child predator
ground rules, 206–7, 251

hard drive
  backing up, 78, 80, 82, 85–86
  definition, 261
  disposing of, 83, 88
  external, 31, 85, 259
  inappropriate content, 174–75
  searching, 40, 175, 218
  security issues, 79–80
  useful extras, 38
harassment. *See* cyberbullying
home computing. *See* computer
homeschooling, 12. *See also* school
homework help, 182, 238–39
hot spot, 57, 262

identifier broadcasting, 56, 57.
See also ESSID; SSID
identity theft, 42, 43, 46, 220, 223, 262
IM
   child predators, 109, 112, 192
   child use of, 65–66, 124
   cyberbullying, 104, 107, 192
   definition, 263
   find conversations, 218
   issues, 191–92
   parent advice, 112, 192
   privacy, 47, 65, 191
   schools and libraries, 192
   screen name, 65
   software, 191, 214
   See also chat room
inappropriate behavior
   by child, 165
   by child predator, 109–11
   See also inappropriate content
inappropriate content
   controlling, 167–75
   cookies, 172–74
   filtering, 169
   history files, 170–72
   how exposure happens, 164
   Internet use agreement, 168, 248
   issues, 175
   online services, 168–69
   portable data storage, 169
   searching hard drive, 174–75
   seeking, 165
   unwanted email, 130, 138
information requests
   child predators, 109, 112–13
   family privacy rules, 63–64
   online alias, 68–69
   personal information, 46
   responding to, 70–72, 78, 81
Innocent Images Initiative, 115.
   See also FBI
instant message. *See* IM
Internet access. *See* online access
Internet role in family life, 21–22
Internet Explorer
   blocking popups, 55–56
   cookies, 52–53, 54–55, 173–74
   and Firefox, 40
   history files, 170–72

Internet Explorer (*continued*)
   Outlook Express, 217
   See also browser; Windows XP
Internet safety and security resources, 220–22
Internet use agreement
   cyberbullying, 107
   examples, 247–51
   Family Forms Pack, 247
   role of, 25, 26
   general rules, 168, 251
   privacy, 48–49
   schools, 178–79
   security, 82
   values, 25–26
iTunes, 28, 40, 203, 204, 216.
   See also media player

key phrase, 148, 150–51, 155–56, 264.
   See also directory; search
key site
   characteristics, 154
   finding, 154–60
   See also directory; search
keyword, 147, 264. *See also* directory; search
King County Library, 184

laptop computer. *See* computer
law enforcement, 108, 113–15, 116.
   See also FBI
legal issues. *See* child pornography; child predator; copyright; defamation; fair use; online alias; piracy; pornography
librarian
   how to ask questions, 185–86
   role, 183–86, 187, 188
library
   advice for parents, 188
   card, 182, 188
   filters, 184, 186, 187
   First Amendment, 183
   Internet access, 182, 183–84
   Internet use policies, 183–84, 188
   Library of Congress, 231, 234
   pornography, 186, 187
   role, 182–83

Index 281

link
   definition, 98, 264
   email, 120, 131
   finding key sites, 156, 157, 159
   inappropriate content, 167–68
   web site, 144, 145, 159–60, 161
List of Additional Software, 85, 86, 206.
   See also Family Forms Pack
List of Online Activities, 66, 68, 72, 169,
   206, 209. *See also* Family Forms
   Pack
List of Data Storage Devices, 86, 169,
   206. *See also* Family Forms
   Pack
lurker, 193, 265

mailing list, 64, 123, 131, 133–34, 265
managing computer use
   computer setup, 50–60, 83, 207–8
   data, 85–86, 169
   ground rules, 206–7, 251
   online activities, 63–65, 72–74,
      86–87, 105–6, 161, 175, 189–203
   paperwork, 205–6
   See also cookies; email; Family
      Forms Pack; inappropriate
      content; Internet use
      agreement; password; popup;
      privacy; security; user name
math and science resources, 242–43
media player, 34, 216–17, 265. *See also*
   iTunes
medical and health sites, 243–44
mouse, 32, 40, 266

NASA, 95
news and weather sites, 237–38

office application suite, 40, 213, 266
online access
   costs and requirements, 37–39
   libraries, 182, 183–84
   options, 35–36
   schools, 178–79
   See also wireless connection
online alias, 68–69
online bullying. *See* cyberbullying
online publishing
   email address, 133
   personal information, 64–65

online publishing (*continued*)
   See also copyright; cyberbullying;
      defamation; fair use;
      First Amendment; podcast
online resources, 219–46
online services
   administrative email, 123, 133–34
   filters, 169
   signing up, 64–68
   using online alias, 68–69
   See also blog; cookies; directory;
      chat room; email; file sharing;
      IM; photo sharing; search;
      social networking; video
      resources; webcam
online videos. *See* video resources
OpenOffice.org, 40, 213
operating system, 33, 267.
   See also firewall; Windows;
      Windows Vista; Windows XP
Outlook Express
   filters, 61–62, 136–37
   inbox display, 137–38
   signature files, 60
   See also email

parents
   resources, 222–23
   role of, 23–24
   explaining decisions, 27
   values, 26, 27
   See also Internet use agreement
parental controls. *See* filter; ground
   rules; inappropriate content
password
   creating, 66–68
   fraudulent requests for, 71, 78
   Internet use agreement, 49
   managing, 68, 74, 115, 206
   online services, 65, 66
   parental access, 249
   security, 67–68, 73, 76, 77
   Windows XP, 59–60
   wireless connection, 56–57
   See also user name
PDF, 33, 40, 214, 267
phishing, 44, 268. *See also* fraudulent
   schemes
photo sharing, 198–99, 246

photographs,
 child predators, 109, 112–13
 cyberbullying, 104, 107
 defamation, 100
 privacy, 73, 195
 satellite, 234
 social networking, 195
 See also photo organizer; photo sharing; Picasa
photo organizer, 33, 268. *See also* photo sharing; Picasa
photo sharing, 198–99, 246, 268
Picasa, 216. *See also* photo sharing
piracy, 101-2, 268. *See also* copyright
podcast, 18, 88, 201–4, 268. *See also* audio resources; media software
popup
 advertising, 44, 45
 browser settings, 52, 53–54, 55–56, 74
 definition, 269
 fraudulent request, 71
 See also browser
pornography
 accidental exposure, 97–98
 child predators, 110, 111
 definition, 96, 269
 email, 99
 free speech, 95–96, 98
 libraries, 186, 187
 school computers, 179
 See also child pornography; First Amendment
portable data storage
 data backup process, 85
 external hard drive, 31, 79–80
 inappropriate behavior, 165
 inappropriate content, 165, 169
 malicious software, 61
 pornography, 110
 privacy, 44
 See also flash drive; List of Data Storage Devices
presentation manager, 34, 213, 269.
 See also office application suite
privacy
 advertising, 44–45
 advice to parents, 74

privacy (*continued*)
 browser setup, 50–56
 child predators, 113
 children and, 48–49
 cookies, 50–55
 data storage devices, 44
 email, 141
 family privacy rules, 48–49, 64–65
 filter, 61–62
 fraudulent schemes, 43–44, 70–72
 ground rules, 206–7, 251
 Internet use agreement, 247–51
 issues, 42, 47–48
 library, 186, 187
 malicious software, 61
 online alias, 68–69
 Outlook Express, 58, 61–62
 passwords, 66–68
 personal behavior, 46
 popups, 52, 53–54, 55–56
 recognizing problems, 73
 relationship to security, 76–77
 school Internet use, 179
 screen name, 65–66
 secrecy, 47–48
 sensitive data, 42–43
 threats to, 42, 43–46
 wireless network, 36, 56–57
 Seven Steps to Online Privacy, 48–73
 software setup, 50–56, 58–61
 user names and screen names, 65–66
 wireless network, 36, 56–57
 See also blog; chat room; file sharing; photo sharing; social networking; webcam
public domain, 91, 92, 94, 95, 225–26, 270

reference resources online, 233–36
router, 32, 56, 57, 270
rule setting
 child predators, 115–16
 cyberbullying, 107–8
 email, 118–22, 125
 Internet use agreement, 247–51
 libraries, 183–84
 child role, 24–25
 parent role, 23–24

Index 283

rule setting (*continued*)
  philosophy, 19–20
  privacy, 64–65
  schools, 178–79
  user and screen names, 65–66

safety and security resources, 220–22
scam, 43–44, 270
  See also fraudulent schemes
school
  acceptable Internet use, 178–79
  advice, 181
  cyberbullying, 106
  email, 123, 128, 139
  fair use, 92, 94, 95
  filters, 99, 166
  homework resources, 182, 238–39
  laptop use, 180
  online alias exception, 68–69
screen name
  creating and managing, 65–66
  personal information, 73
  privacy, 191
  tracking, 68, 206, 251
  use by child, 65
search
  advanced features, 149–50
  advice for using, 153
  choosing, 151
  defined, 271
  displaying results, 151–52
  filters, 152, 166, 169, 183–84
  Google, 148–51
  hard drive, 174–75, 218
  inappropriate content, 165, 174
  key terms, 147
  limitations, 152
  online resources, 223–25
  refining, 150–51
  technique, 146–51
  within web sites, 145
  See also directory; key phrase; key site; keyword; search box; search engine resources

search box, 148, 149, 173, 271.
  See also search
search engine resources, 223–25.
  See also search

security
  activity review, 86, 209
  computer disposal, 83–84
  computer setup, 83
  data management, 85–86
  definition, 75–76
  fraudulent schemes, 79
  hardware and software, 79–80
  Internet use agreement, 82, 249
  issues, 76, 77–78
  key advice, 87–88
  key threats, 78–81
  online habits, 80–81
  online resources, 220–22
  recognizing problems, 86–87
  related information, 77
  related problems, 77–78
  relationship to privacy, 76–77
  Seven Steps to Online Security, 81–86
  software management, 84–85, 214–15
  See also chat room; child predator; cookies; firewall; fraudulent schemes; IM; privacy; virus; webcam; Windows XP; wireless connection
Seven Steps procedures
  controlling email, 132–41
  inappropriate content, 167–75
  online privacy, 48–73
  online security, 81–86
service mark, 90, 92, 226, 271
Shakespeare, 68, 94, 148, 239, 240
signature block. *See* signature file
signature file, 60, 271
social networking, 194–95, 227, 272
Social Security number, 43, 44, 71.
  See also identity theft
software
  basic and optional, 33–34
  finding, 13–14
  free, 28, 34–35, 63, 211–18, 228, 229, 260
  management, 15, 84–85
  See also browser; chat room; file sharing, filter; firewall; email; IM; media player; office application suite; piracy; privacy; wireless connection

spam, 130, 135, 140, 272
spreadsheet 34, 40, 180.
    See also OpenOffice.org; office application suite
SSID, 56, 272

telephone
    online access, 35
    online alias, 69
    online predators, 116
    privacy, 45, 49, 60, 248

unsolicited email. *See* unwanted email
unwanted email
    categories, 130, 131–32
    controlling, 132–41
    filtering, 136–38
    identifying, 138
    responding to, 139–40
    sources, 131
    stopping, 141–42
    See also attachment; fraudulent schemes; inappropriate content; pornography; spam
user name,
    child predators, 115
    ground rules, 206, 251
    Internet use agreement, 249
    managing, 65–66, 68, 74, 190
    privacy, 49, 64–65, 73
    security, 76, 77
    wireless network, 56, 57

video resources, 197–98, 245–46.
    See also copyright; media player; piracy; podcast; webcam
virus
    privacy protection advice, 74
    recognizing security issues, 86–87
    security software, 214–15
    See also Firefox; firewall; Internet Explorer; Outlook Express; Windows XP

web site
    advertising, 44–45
    advice for using, 161
    copyright, 90–95
    fraudulent requests, 44, 70–72
    key sites, finding, 153–60
    malicious software, 61
    privacy, 64–65, 73
    resources, 220–46
    structure, 146–47
    types, 144–45
    See also cookies; copyright; fair use; free speech; inappropriate content; key site; search
webcam, 78, 113, 116, 200–1, 275
window, 17, 275
Windows, 17, 275
Windows Explorer, 53, 55, 122, 173, 174, 275
Windows Vista, 38, 211, 213, 217
Windows XP
    firewall, 59
    included software, 38, 211, 213, 217
    malicious software, 215
    password protection, 59
    privacy, 63
    Service Pack 2, 58
    software management, 84
    updating, 58
wireless connection
    library access, 187
    definition, 276
    modem, 31
    router, 32
    schools, 180
    security, 36, 45, 56–57, 74, 207
    use by children, 36, 39
    wired connection, 36
word processing. *See* word processor
word processor, 34, 213, 276.
    See also office application suite

COLOPHON

This book was produced using the New Book Model Production System as described by Dan Poynter in his book *Writing Nonfiction*.

Research and Information Gathering
Web: Mozilla Firefox 2.0, Microsoft Internet Explorer 6.0 and 7.0

Writing and Manuscript Building
Manuscript Preparation: Microsoft Word 2000
Typesetting:
- Body text: Book Antiqua 12 pt.
- Chapter Titles: Tahoma 20 pt.
- Glossary: Book Antiqua 11 pt.
- Headers: Tahoma 13 pt. and 10.5 pt., Book Antiqua 12 pt.
- Index: Book Antiqua 8 pt.
- Resources: Book Antiqua 11 pt.

Editing: Arlene Prunkl of PenUltimate Editorial Services, http://www.penultimateword.com

Cover Design: Robert Howard of Bookgraphics, http://www.bookgraphics.com

Design, typesetting, and layout:
Page Layout: Microsoft Word 2000

Conversion
Microsoft Word to PDF: Adobe Acrobat 7.0

Printing
Printing by Alexander's Print Advantage from PDF file; http://www.alexanders.com
Paper: 60# White Offset
Cover: 10 pt C1S, four-color, lay-flat gloss film lamination
Binding: Perfect-bound (adhesive, softcover)

SEND YOUR FEEDBACK

No one book can answer all your questions about the Internet, and this book is no exception. Your feedback will help improve the next edition of this book, and will give the author a chance to answer any of your questions. You can contact the author online, or by email, regular mail, phone, or fax:

- **Online**: http://feedback.speedbrake.com
- **Email**: tcurtis@speedbrake.com
- **Mail**: Todd Curtis, Speedbrake Publishing, 24 Roy St., #302, Seattle WA 98109
- **Phone**: 206-300-8727
- **Fax**: 978-926-8043

LISTEN TO THE PODCAST

Visit the *Parenting and the Internet* podcast for additional information as well as for insights into the latest trends of interest to parents of online children. Feel free to send comments about past shows, or suggestions for future topics.

- **Home Page**: http://podcast.speedbrake.com
- **Subscribe**: Podcast home page or iTunes
- **Comments**: feedback@speedbrake.com

DOWNLOAD THE FAMILY FORMS PACK

Download the Family Forms Pack for sample Internet use agreements, suggested ground rules, and much more at http://forms.speedbrake.com

CONTACT SPEEDBRAKE PUBLISHING

Speedbrake Publishing
24 Roy St., #302
Seattle, WA 98109
206.300.8727
http://orders.speedbrake.com
feedback@speedbrake.com

ORDER FORM

Online orders: http://orders.speedbrake.com
Email orders: orders@speedbrake.com
Fax orders: 978.926.8043 (send this form)
Telephone orders: 206.300.8727 (credit card orders)

Postal orders: Speedbrake Publishing
24 Roy St., #302
Seattle, WA 98109

Please send the following books: I understand that I may return any undamaged book for a full refund, for any reason, no questions asked.

_____

_____

Please send me FREE information on:

__ Other Books __ Speaking Engagements __ Consulting

Name _____

Address _____

City _____ State _____ Zip _____

Telephone _____

Email _____

Sales tax: Please add 8.9% for orders destined to the state of Washington.
Shipping costs: Please add $5 for the first book and $2 for each additional book. Book shipments made to US addresses only.
Payment: Payments by check or money order for mail orders.

Other payment options: http://orders.speedbrake.com.